BUILD YOUR

BEVERAGE EMPIRE

Jorge S. Olson

Carlos López

*To all of you with an entrepreneurial
spirit and a desire to succeed*

Get More Content or Coaching

Beverage Industry Domination

Your next step in the quest for beverage domination is sales and distribution or mentoring.

If you're ready to get your product into Mass Retail Accounts all over the USA go directly to the course:
www.WholesaleMBA.com/course

If you need help from me now; in coaching, mentoring and consulting, call today in the USA:

USA Phone: +1 (619) 730-1473

Table of Contents

Introduction

....

Build Your Beverage Empire!

What are your expectations for creating and launching a beverage company? What information and experience do you need to achieve your goals? How can you shorten your learning curve? These all should be your personal goals not only for your new beverage venture but for how this book can help you achieve your short term and long term goals.

Yes, you need to know very specific information such as beverage development costs or how to land your perfect distributor, but the problem is not in what you know, the problem is in what you don't know that you don't know. In the annoying problems that you'll face that are the unknowns in the industry, those you learn by making mistakes. I'll let you in on a little secret; there is nobody as good as making mistakes as I am. I can make a large amount of mistakes in a very short time.

The perfect mentor – I've mentored hundreds of beverage entrepreneurs in the last ten years. This book is now a collection of terms, mistakes, failures, successes, best practices and information from not only my experiences but those experiences from hundreds of new beverage entrepreneurs as well as seasoned beverage executives, distributors and retailers. Like a good mentor, I'll tell you the good, the bad and the ugly. What to do as well as what not to do. I will be firm in some cases and I'll coach you in others.

You'll find the book will tell you different things at different moments in your beverage venture. In the beginning, it will show you how to get started and save time and money. Once you have your product in the warehouse it will show you how to find your best distributor and retailer, and in growth mode you'll hear how to manage growth and cash flow and establish better loyalty programs across the supply chain.

Is there a secret formula for starting a beverage company?

What if someone could tell you the secret formula for creating a beverage that will sell, how to sell it and what it takes to take it nationally from San Diego to New York?

What if you also knew the mistakes newest beverage entrepreneurs make and how much each of them spent in time and money as well as their success rate. This way you could make your budget, avoid all costly mistakes and all that wasted time.

Yes, you'll have this information in this book and much more; and yes, there is a formula for creating a beverage that will sell instead of one that just tastes good. How about we start with that information right here in the beginning of the book so you don't have to wait a few hours to get to the good part?

So what is the correct way to develop your beverage? How can you create a disruptive product and create an instant best seller nationwide? The strategy is actually very easy but counterintuitive. You have to stop researching the internet, stop visiting stores, and start visualizing exercises.

No, imagination and visualization your way to beverage success is not the theme of this book, that's not the type of visualization I mean. You see, most people think of a product and then start researching the ingredients, then formula and production. This is actually the worst thing you can do. You have to start entirely the opposite way. You have to start with the end of the story, with your client happily enjoying your product at his house, or in a bar, or at the beach. This consumer is your ticket to beverage empire heaven. You have to understand everything about this person, how they think, how much money they make, where they shop, their age, sex, and everything about them. You will then find how to motivate them, how to make them try your product and buy it not once, as that doesn't constitute a client, but to buy it several times and become a loyal customer, or even an alpha consumer – that special consumer that tells everyone they just have to buy your products.

This consumer is the basis for your beverage empire. Yes, you will need the right retailer and the right distribution, but even with the best beverage distributors and 7-Eleven, Wal-Mart and Kroger taking your product you won't survive without your consumer. On the other hand, if you find a perfect consumer with the product they need you don't need to worry much about your supply chain as it will come to you.

So how do you find and sell to your perfect consumer over and over again? You do it by developing an emotional connection with them! Yes, you'll probably need innovation and a value proposition to get noticed, but it's not as important as establishing an emotional connection. Remember most if not all buying decisions are based on emotions, so naturally you need to make emotional connections with your audience or customer base to turn your great tasting beverage into a great selling beverage.

After you develop an incredible marketing plan for an emotional connection with your consumer you'll work on your value proposition and selling proposition. On how to be different and show consumers, distributors and retailers that you're different, better, unique. In other words, "don't be a copycat"; don't just think of the same old product with a different label, or a different size, or a different ingredient or flavor. For example, if you're creating an energy drink don't do an 8 once or 16 once can with a better flavor and aim to compete in bars and convenience stores. This is exactly the definition of a copycat and the market will notice. If you flip the energy drink example and create a truly unique value and selling proposition you create a brand new delivery system for your beverage, much like 5-hour energy did with their packaging in a 2 once shot going for $2.99 and shocking the marketplace with a brand new category, you forget about distributors and forget about convenience stores and bars altogether. Maybe you sell with MLM or with Direct Response selling directly to consumers by the case. Any combination of these examples will qualify your product as a disruptive consumer good.

So What's New?

The more things change the more they stay the same! Much has changed since I first wrote this book with Carlos in 2009. This brand new version of the book is updated not just with experiences and projects from the last years, but with the new changes and buzzwords that changed in the industry. A few years ago the buzz was New Age Beverages, now we refer to the same category as "functional", a category that exploded with the arrival of Red Bull and then the other energy drinks like Monster and Rockstar followed by the raging success of VitaminWater and even energy shots, coconut waters and tea's. The new growing category is called "Functional -RTD Tea- Bottled Water" but to make it easier we'll refer to it as "New Age Beverages" or "NAB". In it we'll also include all the new alcoholic beverages such as microbrews, energy malt beverage, flavored spirits and newcomers such as new exotic wines and other spirits from regions across the world such as Mescal from Oaxaca, Mexico. This will facilitate reading and include all the new and exciting beverages with exotic ingredients from the Amazon, Africa, or India.

Even more changes happened in business modeling and the approach to selling products in stores. You'll see a lot of consolidation of products in the refrigerator doors and far less independent products in convenience stores; but don't despair; we've seen new doors open up in supermarkets, the natural category such as Whole Foods and other targeted sales channels. The entire natural category has taken everyone by storm – from natural sodas to organic Amazonian fruit juices and extracts, the door is wide open for you to discover the newest, coolest superfood and squeeze it into a bottle ready for the shelve in natural organic stores.

The emergence of merger and acquisition teams at Coca Cola and the other large beverage companies and investment firms is great for new beverage entrepreneurs. You now have more companies looking for small successful beverages with a bit of traction to invest in them, buy or even take public. These investors don't usually look for ideas, they look for traction, this means your product is made and tested with a few distributors and accounts.

Another notable change, and the one I like the most is Social Entrepreneurship. This is not only new to the beverage industry but to business. I'm personally a social entrepreneur, and I invite you and challenge you to become one yourself, to be part of something even bigger than dollars, than self-success, but success at a greater scale, success for yourself, your family, and expand it from there. Use your business to make a community thrive, or to fund a school, or by simply donating a portion of your winnings. Social Entrepreneurs are dreamers and they don't accept reality, they want to change it, and they use business and the economy as their primary tool.

One thing has stayed the same. The approach to product development and innovation are same best practices that you found years ago are still in place today. Start with your target market and work backward, don't just copy a product with a different formula, contact distributors and retailers before production, create a best value proposition and a best-selling proposition and tie it all up with the packaging that targets your perfect consumer but is distributor and retailer friendly. I know, it's a lot of terminology, but that's why you have a full section of the book dedicated to product development alone.

Who Should Read This Book

Would you be surprised to know that the majority of people that start a beverage company are not from the beverage industry? This poses an ingesting conundrum, as most of you have to start from scratch in the industry without having two, or five, or ten years of experience before you dive into beverage entrepreneurship. Even if you're a salesperson or merchandiser or marketing manager in the beverage industry you'll know something, if you're a salesperson for Pepsi or Coke or Miller beer you know how many accounts you can visit per day for convenience stores, supermarkets or on premise accounts such as bars or restaurants. You also know how to list new products into existing accounts and the amount of time and energy it takes to do this. This experience would serve you well when going after new accounts or calculating sales per store per month. If you're a merchandiser you know how to fight for shelve and refrigerator space and how to keep the store manager happy and the products in front of the consumer at all times. You also know how to place as much point of sale material as possible in and out of the store. You might place poll signs outside, stickers on the refrigerator door and posters on the windows.

Being a veteran employee from the beverage industry doesn't guarantee success as a beverage entrepreneur. Remember as an entrepreneur you're entering the big picture side of the industry. You have to think like a general, not a frontline soldier; not even a sergeant! You have to learn to be a CEO.

If you this is your first entrepreneurship venture you also have to learn how to be an entrepreneur, how to manage risk, expectations and, like any great entrepreneur, how to make things happen. Yes, you have to get as much experience in the beverage industry, but don't underestimate the power of learning marketing, management and entrepreneurship. Get mentors, take courses and read as many books as you can on business subjects. It will pay off.

Who Should Read This Book?
- *New Beverage Entrepreneurs*
- *Existing Business Owners*
- *Wholesalers and Distributors*
- *Salespeople at Beverage Companies*
- *Beverage and Consumer Goods Executives*
- *Formulators, Developers, Co-Packers*
- *Mergers & Acquisitions Managers*
- *Beverage Investors and Analysts*

We wrote this book the first time around strictly for entrepreneurs launching their beverage. After the book was published I received calls from senior management at Coke, Red, Pepsi, SAB Miller, Unilever and other large and small companies as well as distributors, wholesalers and students from many universities; the most surprising conversations where the conversations with existing beverage professionals. They got as much from the book as new entrepreneurs.

This time around I'm also writing for the newcomer, but I'm including much more high level information that veterans will appreciate. This was after much thought, as my editor wanted me to write an entirely new book for the beverage industry, a beverage MBA type book. At the end I decided to make to book much larger and include the two books in one, so you'll have the 101 courses all the way up to the MBA all at the same time. After all, when you're an entrepreneur you need all the help you can get.

So who should read this book? Entrepreneurs will still get the most juice from the book, as they have the most to gain and the most to lose from the industry. An entrepreneur can spend two years and $200,000 learning what you'll learn in a couple of days (or weeks) reading the book. Yes, managers and existing beverage executives will get something from the book, but they don't have their savings at stake like entrepreneurs usually have.

Unbounded Growth & Opportunity

The beverage industry has been growing tremendously in the New Age, Functional and even Alcoholic Beverage Categories. That growth knows no bounds, either. Sales and projections continue to prove that beverages are a solid business to be in—one that only grows by the year, even as some of the most relied-upon, popular drinks start to dwindle and fade. As those products fade, they are being replaced by something bigger, something better, something consumers just can't get enough of; a whole new category of beverages that includes Energy Drinks, Vitamin Water, High End Water, Iced Coffees, Natural Sodas, Energy Shots, Tea's, specialty and microbrewer beers, and the rise of new spirits from Mexico and Eastern Europe and many more (and many just waiting to be developed by eager, prepared developers just like you!). What was new and innovative when I first wrote this book only a few years back is now old news, and raising companies like Fuze, Red Bull, Monster, Rockstar, Izze, Fiji Water and others are now household names. Some of them lead the category, others already sold to companies like Coca-Cola for incredible valuations.

This book is your way—your vehicle, your means, your comprehensive guide to success in the beverage industry.

This book was written specifically for people like you. It was written to show the thousands of entrepreneurs and investors what it takes to successfully produce, launch, sell, and make money in the new age beverage business, all the while building a sustainable business that has what it takes to succeed long-term.

Parts of the Whole Story

In order to best organize the information for your beverage MBA you'll notice the book is arranged into three main parts. In part one, you'll be introduced to the beverage world and why this is the business to invest your time and money in. You'll see how the beverage marketplace currently operates and prepare you to becoming an entrepreneur and CEO in the beverage industry.

In the second part of the book you will go further into the behind-the-scenes world of Beverage Development and tell you exactly how to create a beverage of your own. Here you'll learn the mechanics of producing a beverage from start to finish, as well as the costs associated with it. From start to finish and everything in between, you'll know more about beverage development than 99% of the people in the beverage industry.

The final part of the book will round out the picture and give you the most important piece of the puzzle—the information you need to write and implement a solid business plan. This final part talks about the entire marketing process and how to get sales and distribution, how to approach beverage distributors and retail accounts; get reorders of the product, and then how to sell it off the shelves to those willing consumers. This is the part of the book that will make or break your venture and your future. This is the one part of the business that the vast majority of producers and investors never "get", and that is why most producers will fail.

BUILD YOUR BEVERAGE EMPIRE

PART 3
- Marketing
- Sales
- Distribution
- Retailers and Consumers

PART 1
- Defining your Niche.
- Your Size and Profit.
- Opportunity on the Market.
- Types of Drinks

PART 2
- Developing and Launching.
- Costs and Product Development.
- Target.
- Package, Taste and Ingredients.
- Production & Logistics

CONQUER THE BEVERAGE WORLD

Diagram 1 – Three Parts to the Beverage Book

In the book I'll talk about me, us, we; when it's I, it means me, Jorge Olson, when it's us, or we, it means Carlos and myself or my team that consists of beverage project managers, salespeople, formulators, analysts, brokers, co-packers, and management. Just thought I would clarify!

Your Future Is Bright

That is an outcome that does need to be yours, for one simple reason—you have this book! You have in your hands now a book that puts it all out there for you. A book that collects all that we've learned as successful beverage consultants, entrepreneurs, distributors, retailers and business incubators; a book that makes clear why some drinks fail and others go on to be unmitigated successes; and a book that lifts the veil of confusion, making success in this business not only a real opportunity for you, but a real possibility.

By the end of this book, you will be ready not only develop an excellent Beverage, but also to sell it through and turn it into a profit-producing machine! Your future and your business are waiting, so let's waste no more time. It's time to Build your Beverage Empire!

PART ONE

OVERVIEW OF THE
NEW BEVERAGE
MARKETPLACE

Chapter 1

....

How Much Profit Is There in This Business?

There is definitely a lot of money to be made in the beverage industry; but what we find is that many people with great drink concepts fail because they do not answer the most pressing questions first, and so do not know how to properly plan their new age beverage empire. Before you can decide on whether to invest time, money, and effort in this industry, you first have to know where success in the beverage industry can take you.

The Most Frequently Asked Question in the Biz

In our work with new beverage entrepreneurs we hear one question more than any other: "How much will it cost to launch my new beverage?" And although it is certainly important to know what you are looking at in terms of cost and investment, there are other important factors to consider.

Cost and investment are irrelevant if you do not also know what the potential for return on that investment is; so instead of broaching the question of cost first, we prefer to look at the other end of the equation; first we pose the question, "how much profit can be made by starting, and selling a beverage company?"

It's without question that you have to set your goals first. As any venture capitalist or investment will ask you, "what is your exit strategy and financials". In other words, what's your goal? How much money will you company sell in year one, two and three? How much profit? Once you reach a scalable model, will you sell your business or is this a project you want to keep for many years to come?

As you read the book get your notepad ready, or your computer or tablet! Write down how much you want to sell the first three years of operation and what you think your profit margin on the sale of your products should be as well as your net profit. Do it as a big picture exercise for now, don't get into the details of monthly profit and loss at this time.

Now that you have your big picture goals let's look at what the market looks like at the moment. For that we need to look at two things:
1. How much profit margin you can make as the brand owner?
2. The size and breadth of the beverage industry

So as not to complicate matters, let's start by talking about profit margins and some general numbers you can use to see how much you might personally profit from a New Beverage product or line of products. Let us discuss the size of the beverage industry.

Profit & Margins in Beverage Production

First, a fact; when a beverage—any beverage—is selling at a price between .79 and .99 cents to the consumer that is when that particular industry is considered "cold" (as in, is not growing and profiting significantly). This is the case for many carbonated beverages (sodas) today. A quick trip downtown to the corner convenience store will show you that this is certainly not the case for energy drinks, tea, coconut water, vitamin waters and other functional beverages; many of these are selling at a minimum price of $1.00, many others in the $1.50 to $1.99 range and some go even $2.99 or even higher depending on where you shop. When your product is selling at a price that high, that's when we say *"you're hot!"*

Energy drinks and functional beverages have some of the largest profit margins and repeat sales in consumer products at every level of the sales ladder. This is one of the biggest reasons the Functional Beverage category has become so popular today. It's true that it is also enjoying rapid growth, but more importantly, the profits being made in New Age and Functional Beverages are tremendous.

To give you an example of the potential and profitability let's take the functional beverages as an example picking on energy drinks as they are fairly evenly priced across the board; we'll break down the average costs of production and sales prices for our energy drink

Let's start with some numbers.

Typically, it costs around $7 or $8 to produce a case of energy drink of 24 cans with 16 ounces of liquid per can. That same case has the potential to sell for $24 to a distributor; there is also the potential to sell it directly to the retailer at a price of $32 per case, or directly to the consumer (through a website or mail order) for $48 per case. These prices are in large scale production, minimum production runs can cost $12 per case. In our example we're using 24 cans per case. You have to start thinking in prices and costs by the case not by the can or bottle, as this is how distributors and retailers will buy from you.

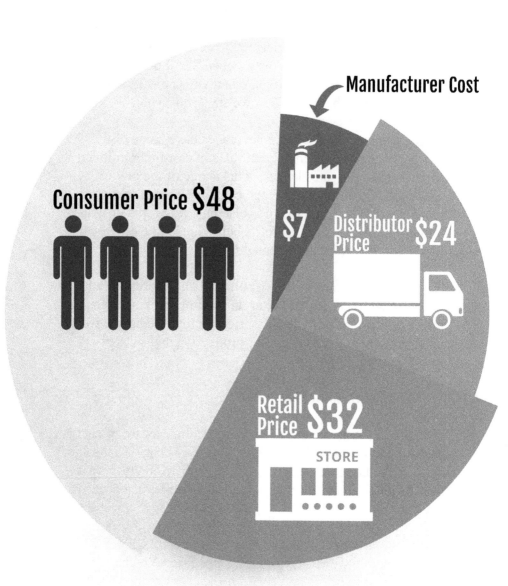

Diagram 1.1 – Costs from Manufacturing to the Consumer

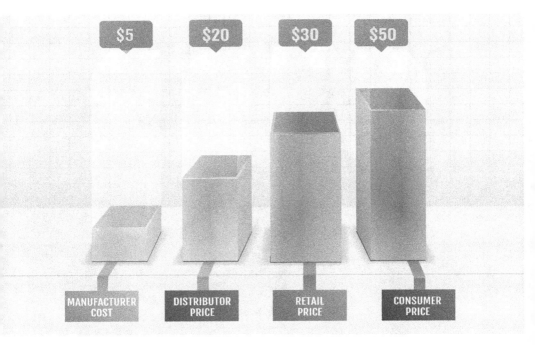

Diagram 1.2 – Supply Chain Cost of Functional Beverages

Taking the example of the $7.00 production cost per case, you can make $17, $25, or even $41 per case! These numbers have the potential to add up very quickly. Now if you consider that the average truckload of 12 ounce beverages holds more than 2,000 cases, even if you only sell at the distributor level, making sales of $24 per case, there is tremendous potential for profit.

Diagram 1.3 – Cost per Can

Translated into hard dollars and cents, this means you are making a 700% return on investment, or a profit margin of 86%. That is an amazing return that is seen in only a few industries; the beverage industry, however, is one of those few.

When you start with a small run of production it's likely you will not make 86% gross margin. To be healthy you have to calculate a gross margin of at least 50%. Using our same energy drink example, if you're selling your beverage at $24 to beverage distributors your cost can be as high as $12 per case of 24 drinks. If you're using a unique biodegradable bottle or one of a kind, all natural ingredients plus agave sweetener you will not meet these numbers. Now you'll have to decide if the agave, bottle and other ingredients are so unique, of so much value, that you can sell at a higher price. This is what we call a UVP or Unique Value Proposition – something so unique and wonderful that will convince consumers that the value is much more than the price. Now you can sell your product for $2.49 or $2.99 to the consumer.

A great example of a higher priced product in the energy category is 5-hour energy. They completely dominate the marketplace with no close second in the radar. According to Forbes magazine they sell more than $1 billion dollars and have only been around for a few years. They sell their product to the consumer for $2.99 for a 2 once shot, Wow! What a way to compete in the category – can you imagine the conversation? "Let's create an energy drink that's only 2 ounces but let's sell it for a dollar more than the 16 once drinks.

Keep in mind that what you think is valuable might not be valuable for your consumer. If you want to charge $1 more because you are all natural and have agave it might not work. I've worked with at least three of such cases, and it did not work with that single unique value proposition. You have to speak with consumers, distributors and retailers to make sure what you think is valuable is really valuable to them. Imagine spending money in developing and producing your drink only to have distributors or retailers tell you "we already tried that ten times and it didn't work, we don't want your product".

Ready to drink convenience store products can carry the least amount of profit as you can see from our examples.

Nutraceuticals, powdered beverages, shots, wine and spirits can sell for much more profit. The case of powdered beverage and shots is clear. They are inexpensive to make. In the case of spirits, you can choose to compete in the high end tier of Vodka, Tequila or other spirits and make much more than 50% gross margin from the start.

If you have a special high end Vodka with a great unique value and selling proposition such as a flavored or infused spirit, you can sell it for $39.99 with a cost of $6 per case. Even after taking out the distributor price and selling it to restaurants and bars instead of retailers you're making $30 Gross Profit per every single bottle. A case of 6 bottles will put a hefty $180 in your pocket. You don't see these kinds of numbers in nonalcoholic ready to drink products.

An important part of your investigation is pricing and profit. It goes hand in hand with your consumer research and your entire business model. If you're funding is limited, and my limited I mean less than one million, I recommend you start with the natural channel with stores like whole foods, or selling to on-premise like bars if you have alcoholic products such as beer, wine or spirits. In the case you have a non-traditional beverage such as a shot, vial, powder or something similar consider direct response, MLM or other out of the box channels. Without the proper funding, don't go into the traditional market. You will not be able to support distributors or pay for advertising to keep consumers buying your product over and over again.

Weaved into your cash flow strategy or your personal monetary goals for this business you should have an exit strategy or at least a long term strategy as your goal. Are you creating this business to run it for the next twenty years? Or will you sell in as soon as a big beverage company offers you a big check? This is very important because your strategy for growth and operating your business will change depending on these goals. If you would like to grow as fast as possible to and sell your company quickly you'll be more aggressive in growth and re-invest most of your money into that growth. If you are keeping the beverage forever, you'll probably want to grow slowly and get perfect distributors and retailers for your product.

Chapter 2

....

Size of the
Beverage Industry

The entire size of the beverage industry is $1,347 billion according to the report "Research and Markets: Global Beverage Industry 2012-2017" published by Research and Markets. This number is incredible.

The new age and functional drinks market has grown to be a serious competitor in the overall beverage industry. New Age and Functional category is one of the only categories enjoying double-digit growth in the beverage industry. In truth, it is the new age beverage and functional drinks market that is sustaining big beverage companies like Coca-Cola and Pepsi as their carbonated drinks see declines and miniscule, even negative, growth. This is why you've seen a wave of mergers and acquisitions from big companies buying and funding many start-up and medium sized companies.

Size Perspective of the Beverage Industry

New age beverages and functional drinks comprise only a fraction of the industry, but this is the category, in fact almost the *only* category, that is growing and showing more and more potential. The whole of the beverage industry is made up of several categories, including

- Carbonated soft drinks

- Bottled water
- Beer
- Wine and Spirits
- Functional Drinks (such as sports, focus, digestion or energy drinks)
- Ready to Drink (RTD) Teas
- New Age Beverages (natural products, shots, etc.)

As you can see, new age and functional beverages are just one category within the drinks market – many in the industry include several categories in one large one calling it Functional RTD Water and Tea because it encompasses the largest growing categories in non-alcoholic beverages. And while it might seem that the old favorites of soda, beer, water, and wine are too ingrained in the marketplace to leave any opportunity, statistics show that just the opposite is true. It seems people have had enough of sugary soft drinks and are turning to new forms of refreshment, and drinks that can give them more.

If we look at the sales for just the top ten energy drinks alone—bearing in mind that this is just *Energy Drinks*, a sub-category of functional and new age beverages—we get a glimpse of the size and impact of the industry. In 2006/2007, the top ten energy drinks topped well over $743 million in sales, which was a change for the better of about 34.4% over the previous year.[1] In 2013 energy drink retail sales only incremented 6.7% and the top three brands in the USA sold over $7.5 billion dollars.

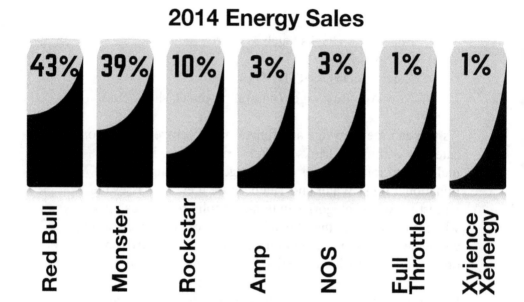

References
1. 2013 Data is from the top brands per, latest 52 week period, Total U.S. Multi-Outlet w/ C-Store (Supermarkets, Drugstores, Mass Market Retailers, Gas/C-Stores, Military Commissaries and Select Club & Dollar Retail Chains) provided by "IRI, a Chicago-based market research firm (@iriworldwide)".

2. 2014 Data is from IRI covering a 52 week period ending November 2, 2014 based on USA sales only and retailers not reporting.

3. Prior to 2013 the data was complied from data published by beverage industry insider. Bevnet.com

Diagram 1.4 – Energy Drink Sales

Now to really put this into perspective we have to point out that these are the numbers for just the top ten energy drinks—names like Red Bull, Monster, Rockstar, Full Throttle, AMP, NOS and Xenergy. These numbers do not even account for the smaller players that are still seeing huge gains and making big profits. And these numbers do not account for the many other types of beverages in growing specialty segments like functional, specialized liquor, wines, vitamin waters, teas, coffees, and many others to consider. Growth figures for the overall energy drink category are now steady at around 7% in the current market with domination from the big players that have run most small energy drink companies out of business. But don't let these numbers bother you as you don't want to compete with Red-Bull, or Coke, or Patron Tequila. You have to find a niche to exploit and create your market right there. Why would you compete with Red-Bull creating another energy drink when they sell more than 5 billion cans worldwide each year with their 8,000 employees? These numbers are here as part as a big picture, to feed your business model as well as your business acumen.

All of these figures and percentages can be confusing, their true impact elusive. So to put things in more understandable terms, let's take a look at another set of numbers for the energy drinks category. Research performed by the Market Research Group has shown that in just five years, the period from 2002 to 2007 when energy drinks really entered the market in the USA, the energy drinks market grew 440%. In dollars and cents that equates to a huge $6.6 billion dollars in sales each year; but energy drinks are not done growing—by 2011, it was projected that energy drinks will top $9 billion in annual sales. That means that for energy drinks alone there was an additional $2.4 billion in sales up for grabs over the next couple of years that was not yet accounted for at that time, and at least $6.6 billion in current sales that could be tapped by new drink products. And again, we're talking about just the opportunity with energy drinks a few years back. At this writing, the top 5 energy drink brands sell almost $20 billion dollars per year according to Euromonitor.

As a whole, the new age and functional category is posting a very impressive growth each year. The functional beverage category has sales in 2015 of $63 Billion year with $17.9 Billion coming from the USA. In the USA you can see a growing trend year after year. This is without considering other new age beverages such as waters, craft beer, liquor and other new products. The functional trend shows in all food, with a global functional food market of $190 Billion according to Statista.

What Do All These Numbers Mean?

Admittedly, the statistics, numbers, and data presented here and in other beverage industry analyses can be quite complex and confusing. What's more, these numbers represent just the tip of the iceberg in beverages reports and statistics; there is much more that can be learned and analyzed. We include this taste of statistical data here just as an example of what the industry promises and what the future of Beverage market is capable of.

However, in addition to the straight facts, which we've done our best to present in understandable and meaningful terms, it helps to understand something about what the data means.

First off what you should know is that this $100 billion (+) figure is the amount of money consumers are paying for beverages in a given year. This is what we as are spending at convenience stores, supermarkets, and so on. It is a retail figure, not some wholesale sales number. This figure represents the actual amount of money that changes hands over counters during retail point of sale transactions. Why don't I provide you with the wholesale number, or the numbers form the sales of manufacturers or brands to the distributors? Because I don't have it. Or more accurately, because I can't get it. Most beverage companies are private companies and don't share their yearly sales.

More importantly, though, what you need to know to gain a perspective on the market and opportunities in the beverage industry is that these figures are based on something known as "scan data." Scan data is the sales figures compiled when you go to the market to buy a product and they hit that bar code with a UPC scanner. Market retailers send their scan data to research companies like Nielsen's, and it is these figures that are used to compile this information.

Now, to take this a step further you need to realize that not all sellers are participating in scan data; only a portion of the retail beverage markets are. Often times liquor stores, bars, and even some big retail giants like Wal-Mart do not participate in scan data, and so their retail beverage sales are not included in this type of reporting. This is why if you read a market report, you will see exclusions such as, "based on scan data not including Wal-Mart."

So what does this mean for the size and opportunity in the new age beverage market?

What this means is that the use of scan data can give us an idea as to the size of the Beverage market, but it is not entirely accurate. In fact, the size of the Beverage market is probably much bigger than what is reflected in reports based on scan data. The feedback that we get directly from manufacturers is that the numbers that are out there simply do not add up; sales are truly more brisk than these numbers. Very simply, Beverages in all categories are selling in even higher numbers.

Scan data has an especially deceptive impact in the Functional, RTD Tea and Bottled Water category because new these drinks sell more at the convenience levels and at small, convenient points of sale like gas stations and small, family-owned stores. These types of places often do not participate in scan data at all, and so there are a large proportion of sales that are missed in many statistics reports.

There is a way to get more complete accounting of the sales in this beverage category, but you have to go directly to the producers or retailers themselves. Call a company directly and they will be able to tell you what their true sales volume is. That being said, these statistics still serve a very useful purpose—they show us that sales of energy drinks and new age beverages are brisk, and that in truth they are even brisker still. In my research for this book I called more than twenty privately held companies to speak about their experiences, strategy, opinions and their sales. They did share sale numbers and other financials but asked not to publish them using their names.

A Growing Business

Rank	2014	2014 Sales ($millions)	2013	2013 Sales ($millions)	2012	2012 Sales ($millions)
1	Red Bull	$ 2,883.00	Red Bull	$ 3,433.00	Red Bull	$ 2,950.00
2	Monster	$ 2,476.00	Monster	$ 3,147.00	Monster	$ 2,600.00
3	Rockstar	$ 647.00	Rockstar	$ 821.00	Rockstar	$ 780.00
4	NOS	$ 294.00	NOS	$ 274.00	Amp	$ 300.00
5	Amp	$ 212.00	Amp	$ 239.00	NOS	$ 250.00
6	Full Throttle	$ 114.00	Full Throttle	$ 104.00	Full Throttle	$ 140.00
7	Xyience Xenergy	$ 40.00	Xyience Xenergy	$ 43.00	Xyience Xenergy	$ 40.00
8	Arizona Energy	$ 28.00	VPX Redline	–	VPX Redline	$ 15.00
9	Rip It	$ 22.00				
10	Venom	$ 19.00				

2012 Sales ($millions)	2011	2011 Sales ($millions)	2010	2010Sales ($millions)	2008	2008 Sales ($millions)
$ 2,950.00	Red Bull	$ 2,300.00	Red Bull	$ 2,200.00	Red Bull	$ 0.40
$ 2,600.00	Monster	$ 1,900.00	Monster	$ 1,500.00	Monster	$ 0.23
$ 780.00	Rockstar	$ 660.00	Rockstar	$ 400.00	Rockstar	$ 0.12
$ 300.00	Amp	$ 330.00	NOS	$ 200.00	Amp	$ 0.08
$ 250.00	Doubleshot	$ 250.00	Doubleshot	$ 180.00	Full Throttle	$ 0.04
$ 140.00	NOS	$ 220.00	Amp	$ 140.00	Doubleshot	$ 0.02
$ 40.00	Full Throttle	$ 130.00	Full Throttle	$ 110.00	NOS	$ 0.02
$ 15.00	Xyience Xenergy	$ 30.00	–	–	No Fear	$ 0.01

2007	2007 Sales ($millions)	2006	2006 Sales ($millions)
Red Bull	$ 0.35	Red Bull	$ 0.43
Monster	$ 0.27	Monster	$ 0.14
Rockstar	$ 0.11	Rockstar	$ 0.11
Full Throttle	$ 0.07	Full Throttle	$ 0.07
Amp	$ 0.05	Sobe No Fear	$ 0.05
No Fear	$ 0.03	Amp	$ 0.04
NOS	$ 0.02	Sobe Adrenaline Rush	$ 0.03
Adrenaline	$ 0.02	Tab Energy	$ 0.02

Diagram 1.6 – US Market New Age Growth

Just a few years ago, this category was posting growths as high as 75%; now it's back to normal growth in the entire category, but this normal market correction simply means that the market is stabilizing and readying itself for the long-haul and steady, sustainable growth and profitability. Once a new product hits the market the category will again blow up!

Nevertheless, when all is taken into account, it is clear that the only portion of the beverages industry with real room for more products and opportunity is the new age beverage industry. With billions of dollars in additional sales projected through the next several years, the place with promise is this still burgeoning and yet continually underserved segment of the refreshment beverage market.

Chapter 3

....

More Opportunities

in the Beverage Industry

Outside of the U.S. beverage market there is even more opportunity to be tapped for New Beverage developers. And for those of you already positioned through your first line of business, the potential in the beverage market could be even greater. Let's not forget the New Age Beverages (NAB) include Functional, RTD Tea, Bottled Water, Shots as well as new alcoholic beverages and any other new and exotic drink coming into the market.

More than U.S. Markets

Up until now we have only discussed the potential for profiting as a producer and seller of a new age drink in the United States or in your home country. Yet just next door could be an even wider-open market that is desperate to see their demands for beverages met.

Many North Americans and USA companies do not realize this, but Mexico is the number two importer of U.S. products in the world behind Canada. And of even more interest to us as producers of drinks, Mexico has a great demand for all types of U.S. beverages, including energy, flavored waters, sodas, shots and all measure of alcoholic beverages. It's a whole new market possibility waiting just next door. In addition, Mexico is a huge beverage consumer; the country is one of the largest consumers of beverage in the world per capita. This includes consumption of soda and beer, but also consumption of energy drinks, flavored waters, and other new age beverages.

But the huge demand for U.S. beverages is not being met in Mexico. Beverage exports to Mexico are underrepresented; only about $147 million worth of beverage exports are going from the U.S. into Mexico each year. This translates into a trade deficit of around $2 billion dollars in beverages each year. According to the U.S. Census Bureau and the U.S. Bureau of Economic Analysis

The demand for these beverages is so great that producers of good NAB's don't have to work hard at all to tap into the Mexican drinks marketplace—Mexicans come into the U.S. looking for these products to export themselves because they simply have no products or production facilities available to them in Mexico. Largely these are big wholesale distributors and big retail outlets buying U.S. NAB's by the truckload. This makes it easy for you to start selling and exporting your NAB to Mexico and start taking advantage of a wide-open, virtually empty market many drink producers are missing.

If you have a good product, these Mexican exporters will eventually find you. You could take the passive route to exporting to Mexico just by

- Getting your Beverage into U.S. trade shows (if you do not go yourself, place a retailer or distributor there to sell, or hire a broker to handle trade shows for you)
- Making yourself easily accessible (include an international telephone number, not just a U.S. toll-free number, on all materials; include email and website address as well, and make sure all of this information

is on everything—product labels, business cards, and brochures, too)
- Having the right information ready and waiting (pre-determine your international price [which is usually lower than your U.S. price, especially if the exporter pays transportation and export fees; you can make up the difference in volume]; know product specifications—weight, dimensions, case count, pallet count)

With a passive approach, your drink could move into the Mexican market in months or years, but with a more active approach you could be selling in Mexico in short order (NOW!). If you do not want to leave anything to chance, and you want to ensure your drink's entrance in to the Mexican marketplace, take a more active approach and

- First learn about your target market (know what consumers are paying for drinks like yours, know the import and transport costs, know the profit margins of distributors and retailers, know where your product can sell and how many of these outlets or stores there are)
- Find customers (enter Mexican trade shows, locate U.S. distributors selling in Mexico, find beverage brokers dealing there)
- Determine what support your new customer-base needs (is a promotional campaign in order to retain sales? do you need to provide retailers with Point of Sale, or POS, materials? are sales commissions in order?)

Taking either an active or passive approach, you can extend your sales, or even target them primarily towards beverage sales in Mexico. Mexico is yet another market that further expands the opportunity of profiting in the NAB industry.

Do You Already Have a Foot Forward?

Some of you reading this book already have a clear advantage over the rest. Some of you out there have a built-in advantage; maybe you're a distributor or retailer, a small independent store, or a seller or developer with a strong online presence selling either beverages or complementary products—maybe something that goes hand in hand with selling NAB's. If you are one of these people or businesses, then that's all the more reason you have to go into the business of producing a new age drink.

For those of you reading this book who already engage in one of these businesses or who have that extra advantage, building a new age drink product line should be all the more attractive because you can eliminate many of the steps and place your own beverage products at the forefront of your sales.

If you are a distributor (and not necessarily just a beverage distributor, although this would be best) you have already established a relationship with retailers and because of that they might help you out. If you've had a good working relationship retailers might get behind your product and really give it that extra push to move it off the shelves.

Many distributors haven't yet woken up to this opportunity, creating their own NAB and distributing it through already established sales channels. These businesses continue to be approached and build up new brands for others only to find that in five or six years they are traded up or down for another distributor and their competition ends up reaping the real rewards of their hard work and sacrifice. For us, as beverage incubators, it's easy to empathize with people in these situations and help them develop their own brands to keep this from happening again. For the distributors, it's easy for them to see the benefit of owning the brand, letting go of those without loyalty and replacing them with the most loyal product developers of all—themselves!

This effect is not limited to distributors, though. The same effect trickles down to the retailers. Retailers, like distributors, also have a lot to do with building brands. Retailers lose space on their shelves to promote new brands. They'll make good money on new products at first because hungry producers will offer them great profit margins of 30 or 40%. Then once these retailers get the drinks selling in high numbers that profit margin is cut and the producer charges the retailer a 5% higher wholesale price. The retailer begins to wonder why they should keep giving up prime selling real estate and shelving to a producer that keeps squeezing him into a smaller and smaller profit margin; he begins to think about moving on to the next new producer to enjoy those bigger profit margins once again. The smart ones start to understand that if that next new product were his anyway, the entire profit margin would be his and it would never be reduced.

People in these sorts of positions have a clear advantage already; truthfully the advantage is in their already established lines of sales and the business to business networking that's been established through the primary business. Readers in these types of positions already know where and how they'll sell their drinks. The benefits are so clear that often we wonder why we don't see more retailers and distributors developing their own new age drinks product line. For those of you who have heard the call, we invite you to get serious about creating your own NAB and tell us all about it.

You Should Own Your Own Private Label

Each distributor, retailer and restaurant or bar owner, and many other business owners, should have his or her own drink. If you are a distributor, retailer, store owner, liquor store owner, restaurant owner, or bar owner you should have your own private label drinks already. If you do not, you are losing money marketing other people's drinks when you could be reaping all the profits yourself, since you already have established sales outlets.

Just as we discussed for distributors, retailers, and hospitality, if you are already in the business in one or more ways the major costs and infrastructure components like sales, transportation, and warehousing are already in place and being paid for. You can produce a number of drinks (like non-carbonated products with no gas) for less than you can buy them from the local distributor. These include drinks like:

- Sports drinks
- Enhanced waters
- Teas
- Wine
- Spirits

By selling your own private label drinks, and producing them at less cost, you can double or triple your profits on similar drinks that you sell for others, possibly even selling at a lower retail cost over others products on your shelves and in your coolers. What's more, you can build a brand for your business through your own label and further promote yourself with every private label drink that walks out your door.

Getting on Board with New Opportunities

The sales statistics, the unaccounted sales data, and the thirsty markets inside and outside the U.S. prove that the time of the new beverages has arrived. All alcoholic and non-alcoholic NAB's are the *hot* drink product, the only one with promise today. If you are positioned with even greater advantage through marketing, sales, or distribution, the opportunity for quickly profiting from the NAB craze is greater still.

Everyone is looking for new age beverages—consumers know what they are and they are looking, bottlers are looking for more bottling business, distributors and retailers are looking to enhance their product offerings and their sales and bars and restaurants look for new wines and spirits to serve younger clients. The new age drinks market is big business, and it's only getting bigger.

Chapter 4

....

Learning From Mistakes

You'll learn from your mistakes, but you'll also learn from our mistakes and all the mistakes form our clients, projects and companies.

We're very enthusiastic to share the growth and success of the industry with you, and show you, as we did in the last chapter, how great an opportunity the beverage market is. But to be fair to our readers, we also have to talk about the failed products and companies we've seen over the years because learning to successfully develop and sell your new beverage requires that you're also aware of the potential pitfalls that new market entrants regularly fall into.

Yes, I know what you're thinking. 90% of new businesses fail within the first year. So that's normal in any business. Yes it is, however there is no need to go through the fail cycle in the beverage industry, it can be avoided, and that's what makes failure so ugly.

Winners & Losers in the Beverage Industry

We can say without a doubt that the number of entrepreneurs that have failed in this business is far greater than the number of those that came out winners.

In 2014 my team spoke with more than 300 new beverage entrepreneurs determined to create a beverage and be incredible successful in the business. We had several conversations with each one of these entrepreneurs, some of them even worked with us in their project.

As part of a survey we stayed in contact with all of them and at the end of 2014 we found out most of them where out of business. Before we jump to conclusions we have to study how committed these 300 entrepreneurs and companies really were to creating a beverage business.

When we spoke with them for the first time and subsequent times, all 300 told us they were 100% committed to their business. However many of them did not have funding, did not know how to get funding, and did not know how much money they really needed to start a business. We all have several ways of interpreting this information:
- They are not 100% committed and it's just an idea
- They will create their company anyway
- They just wanted a barrier to stop their project

I'm sure we can come up with many more interpretations but let's stick to these three for our example. The fact is (what we know for sure) is that every one of them wanted, and told us they wanted to start a company. The reality is that 50% stopped perusing their project after the first thirty days, and only 10% finished an actual beverage concept. A beverage concept means they have their formula, artwork and samples but no sales or real inventory. Of those 30 people that created their beverage only one of them is in stores at the moment. The other 29 did not really open any stores, or they opened and lost the few stores they did open, or they did not get a distributor, or they ran out of money.

I saw this for the first time in a large scale back in 2007 when more than 200 new energy drinks entered the market. Almost anywhere you go you can see remnants of these once exuberant producers; many of these products, however, just sat on warehouses, on supermarket shelves, and in the trunks of the cars of hundreds of sales reps nationwide. Despite the biggest dreams and best intentions of high profits, these drinks failed for some very simple and common reasons. It's a common occurrence we call the "bad and the ugly" of the drink industry. This ugly side of has a little to do with suppliers and representatives taking advantage of these enthusiastic drink producers, but it has mostly to do with something as simple as basic planning and commitment.

Managing Risk – Avoid Failure

We now know that hundreds of drink producers fail every year; but why? Why didn't these products sell? Why did these people—once determined and full of great ideas and ambition—fail?

There are endless reasons why great drinks and motivated entrepreneurs fail with their beverages, but more than anything these drinks failed because of a lack of basic planning. These developers went about marketing and selling their drinks in all the wrong ways; it's something we've seen so often we've even named the problem—reverse engineering.

Reverse engineering happens when developers start at the end—the end product and assumed end sales to consumers—without first creating a basic plan for development, distribution, and marketing.

In our business as beverage entrepreneurs, investors and incubators, we see this all too often. Too many people come to us after having started their beverage without doing the research first. They start with the easy part—developing the actual beverage. Making your own beverage is not really hard. People come to us and tell us that they have a great

concept or flavor; they think their drinks will just sell themselves because they have
1. The best tasting drink, or
2. The best looking drink, or
3. The best logo or bottle

Let us tell you there are a *lot* of best tasting and best looking drinks out there--and many of them are going nowhere! Let us be the first to tell you that it is not enough to have the best looking or tasting drink. In fact, many drinks succeed without good taste and good looks. Just look at the big-seller energy drinks that are out there, like Red Bull; need we say more?

We get these calls and emails all the time; and we tell every one of them the same thing—it's not just about creating your drink. We go on to ask these people the right questions that will help them sell:

- Who are your distributors?
- How will you sell your drink?
- What POS or advertising will you offer the retailer?

With just 30 seconds of due diligence we find out that this product is destined to hit the 99 cent store inside of a week. Yet still, these developers insist that they don't need to know this information because their product is just so great the selling and marketing will take care of itself.

Some people go so far as to create drinks without having an inkling of who the product is for. All of this really matters because it determines how you package your drink, where you will sell it, and how you will market it and promote it. After all, a drink intended for runners isn't going to be packaged in a glass bottle with a metal top. These are the types of things we try to point out to our callers and customers to show them how they need to be thinking about their products before they start producing them.

From here it gets even uglier because with ignorance and poor planning comes the potential for these developers to be taken advantage of. The suppliers who are selling to producers 8,000 cases of bottles, tops and labels don't care whether these drinks really ever take off--not so long as they already have their cash in-hand. So they'll continue to sell the products, services, and supplies these developers will pay for and these entrepreneurs will continue to get taken.

We try our hardest to educate all of the callers and emailers to help them see how they really need to start the drink development process at the beginning—to see that mixing a batch of a great tasting drink is not enough. But with such a great opportunity as this the calls become unmanageable, and so instead we've decided to put it all down in this book and in our audio course to give you a reliable reference and insight into the world of new age drinks.

For Want of a Basic Business Plan

Think about it this way. If you were to build a ten-story building, would you try to do it without a good set of plans drafted from a skilled, experienced engineer? Would you just start mixing concrete and hammering nails, waiting to see where it takes you? No. You would start with a definite plan, and a well thought-out, carefully designed blue print.

Developing and launching a new beverage is really no different. The business is about much more than simply developing a great tasting product. So as a beverage developer without inside knowledge and industry experience, why would you attempt to produce a drink without professional guidance and a solid business plan, or without an experienced and knowledgeable engineer to guide you? You need to hire an experienced team starting with management, or get advice from people who already succeeded in the industry.

To start you need to develop at least a basic business plan that outlines who your product is for, how you will get it to them, how you'll get them to buy it, and how you will land and support distributors and retailers. If you want to get more technical, include your Unique Selling and Unique Value Propositions as well. Of course, this is a simplified version of what it takes to write a business plan and successfully launch a new beverage; we'll talk more in depth about business plans in a later chapter. However, what we really need to get across here in the beginning is that if you do not have such a plan you will almost certainly fail.

Developing a new beverage is not just about mixing flavors and features; it's about knowing how you will sell that end product to

- Distributors
- Retailers
- End consumers

Probably 99.9% of drink developers forget this basic principle, and that is why so many of these drinks fail—for no better reason than the developer failed to think through their product and appeal, planning for its delivery and sale from the beginning.

You Need To Hire a Team!

There you have it, the rest of the picture. Now you know the good, the bad, and the ugly as each applies to developing a new age drink. It's not always a pretty picture, but we beg you not to let this deter you from becoming the next successful name in the new age or energy drink market.

You see, it's not that this is so difficult an opportunity to take advantage of, it's just that you have to go about it in the right way. You have to start at the beginning; you have to do your research and planning; you have to know all facets of the industry—the good, the bad, and the ugly; and you need to get professional help for those aspects that are beyond you.

You wouldn't build that ten-story building without an engineer, and you should not think about launching your beverage without the help of a professional team and a solid business plan. A professional team will talk you through and guide you through every phase of the process, helping you evaluate and answer the essential questions like "how to" and "how much" as they apply to everything from product concept and development to warehousing and logistics, to sales and marketing.

To get your team you have a few options. You can hire a COO, VP or other employee to help you with your product or you can hire a consultant while you're in the start-up phase. Consultants will charge you by the project or on a monthly basis. I take a few projects per year and charge on a monthly basis more as a mentoring method. I found this is what is better for entrepreneurs. This way they can learn how to be a beverage CEO while working on their immediate deliverables. In most cases that'sbeverage development and business model.

Chapter 5

....

The New Era of Beverage

From sales to valuations, X Games, Mixed Martial Arts (MMA), and beyond, this industry is hot—*very* hot. And like any other industry, product, fad, or fashion, there is a window of opportunity that is open for only a certain, unknown period of time. When that window closes, it will be time to start looking for the next wave of opportunity. For those of you reading this book now, the window into the beverage market is still wide open, and all indicators tell us we still have time.

What Market Indicators Are Saying

We look at these many industry and market indicators, and we see that this is still a growing segment of the beverage industry with plenty of profit left for the taking. We've touched on these indicators in other chapters, such as the chapter on the Size of the Beverage Business, but let's take a minute to recap and consider them from the perspective of not just business size, but also from the point of view of the opportunity that creates.

This list includes just the current and projected sales figures. Let's also remember that we have at our disposal:

- A U.S. beverage market of at least $100 billion per year
- Unaccounted sales not included in Scan Data statistics which further bolster profits and potential

- A wide-open Mexican drinks market, thirsting for U.S. beverage products

We look at this larger picture, and we sense a theme. We sense that the markets in the U.S. and in Mexico are ripe now for profiting in the new age drinks market. We sense that this is without a doubt the new era of beverages.

Demand, Profit, Potential

Market indicators are one of the first places to start when you want to evaluate the potential within a given market. But there is more of a story to be told, one that is not so easily measured but that is apparent to those out in the field and in the trenches.

In addition to the proven sales, there is also a great and growing demand for NAB products. And not only is there a growing demand for these fashionable and trendy drinks, but there is also a demand for the newest and best the drinks market has to offer. Consumers are looking for the drink that can give them more, more, more…a simple solution in a bottle.

Right alongside of this we have a great potential for profit and large profit margins. Where there is profit to be made, entrepreneurs like you will follow. But after a time, the market becomes flooded and the potential for profits is lost.

Both demand and profit are subjects that deserve a discussion all of their own, and we will do that in the next chapter; however, these are also factors that are essential to determining when the new era of a product might be, and both of these indicate that the era of the Beverage Business is now.

Business Values & More

Another topic that we'll delve into in a later chapter, which also applies here, is business valuations. The values of established and successful new drinks companies are soaring, and some unprecedented sales have been made. This is something else we can look towards as an indicator of the arrival of the NAB era, and as an indicator of open opportunity. As you read about the specific sales and valuations of new age beverage companies in a later chapter, keep this in mind; understand that the high values of these companies and the resulting big-dollar sales can only be taken as confidence in the demand, profitability, sustainability, and long-term performance of beverages.

Essential Resources, All in a Row

In order for an era of beverages to truly be established, to be considered in full-swing, a number of factors all need to align. One of those factors is the readiness of essential market resources at all points on the spectrum. Right now, all the essential resources from development to production to consumers are aligned, which means that the timing is perfect to enter into this field now.

Let's take a detailed look at these essential resources that you now have at your disposal, ready and waiting for your drink; they include:

- Flavor companies or Ingredient Houses
- Manufacturers
- Bottlers
- Retailers
- Distributors

And most importantly

- Consumers

The flavor companies or ingredient houses are tuning in to the new possibilities in drink flavorings; they now understand that it's not just about artificial and sticky sweetness anymore. They are increasing their lines and enhancing additives to include vitamins, minerals, herbs and botanicals, fruits, organics, and much more. They are also more open now to pursuing new flavor lines that have never been tried before. Flavor companies are ready to partner with you to become the innovative leaders in their field.

Manufacturers of drink supplies are also coming on board. They are coming to understand the appeal of unique packaging, of the sexy and the sleek, of the practical and solution-oriented drink supply product. From bottles to caps to wrappers and labels, supply manufacturers are ready to lead, too.

Bottlers are in line, happy for the increase in business to mix and package new age drinks. A number of bottlers have also expanded their capacity to handle unique bottling needs, including the needs of producers packaging natural and organic drinks and hot- and cold-fill products. No longer do you have to wait for a bottler to develop the processing for your drink, you simply need to locate the right bottler who is already capable of handling your drink.

Retailers and distributors are, naturally, interested in stocking the drinks that are hot, the products that will sell. From experience they know that right now the products they can move and make big money on are the new age beverages and that without them their sales will be very disappointing.

Consumers are the most important resource to have in line because, as you know, these are the people who will be buying your drink. Consumers now are educated and accustomed to trying out new beverage products; they've seen what they can get and they want more. For those drinks entering the market today there is no learning curve like what the pioneers in the market endured. Earlier products had to wait for consumers to warm to new beverages, but your drink will come into this educated market and will be readily recognized for what it is. Better still, your drink will come into the market in the next phase—the phase where consumers want the products, but want new beverages that will do even more. Now consumers are waiting to see what the next era in new age beverages will usher in to meet their needs and demands better and more tastefully.

Before Time Runs Out

Without question we are in the midst of the new era of beverage now; but the era will not last forever; or at least, the opportunity in the new era will not last forever. As the players get bigger it will be harder and harder to capitalize on the opportunity this era presents.

As the industry grows, and as more and more players give the big drink companies (the Coke, Pepsi's of the world) a run for their money, the big contenders work harder and harder to squeeze the industry and block new competitors from taking away from their market.

Big drink companies are beginning to clue in to the fact that there is a lot of opportunity for small drink producers, and that these drinks producers (you!) can mean serious competition with new and innovative, *better*, new drinks. They are also starting to block competition by cornering bottling, distribution, and retail outlets.

The demand for these products is not going away; the wave of new beverages is swelling and swelling, continuing on the move. And there is great opportunity within this market, but you have to get on board now before the big names have their way with it. The time to start a beverage company is now.

Chapter 6

....

Why Functional &

Beverages are Hot

Today's consumers have more options than ever before. Anywhere they go they can choose any beverage they want. There is a beverage to fit every lifestyle, delivered in a variety of sizes, prices, packaging, colors, and even smells. And today's consumer is clearly driven. He will buy what he wants in order to "feel" how he wants. How else can you explain why people are willing to pay $1.99, $2.99, $3.99, or even more for nicely packaged water, soda, energy drinks, energy shots, coffees, and other beverages?

Why Functional Beverages Are Hot—Profit

Functional Beverages and New Age Beverages are hot from the perspective of both producers and consumers. From the standpoint of producers they are hot for primarily one reason—profit, and lots of it.

Drink developers get into the business because there is money to be made, plain and simple. The potential for sizeable profit margins are a major driver in this industry. To revisit that, let's review the potential profit for the category.
- Cost of production per case = $6 to $10
- Wholesale sales estimate per case = $24

- Mid- and high-level [retail] sales estimate per case = $32 to $50 , respectively
- Direct to consumer price estimate = $1.49 to $2.99/unit

So here again we see the potential for gross profit in the functional category:

- Per case at lowest wholesale price = $18
- Per case at mid- and high-level sales = $25 and $41, respectively
- Direct to consumer profit per case (assuming case size of 24) = $40 /average per case

These numbers are impressive, but it's still difficult to foresee the potential in profit in terms of volume; this number will, of course, depend on how much of your drink you move—how many retail outlets you have for it and how well it sells. However, just to give you an idea, consider that every truckload of beverage contains approximately 2,000 cases. So for every truckload of product you sell your gross profit numbers may look like this:

Selling to distributor:

- 2,000 cases/truck
- x $17 profit/case
- = $34,000 gross profit per truckload

Selling to retailer:

- 2,000 cases/truck
- x $25 profit/case
- = $50,000 gross profit per truckload

Selling directly to end consumer:
- 2,000 cases/truck
- x $41 profit/case

o   = $82,000 gross profit per truckload

Diagram 1.7 – Profits per truckload

Minimum Gross Profit Potential per Truckload

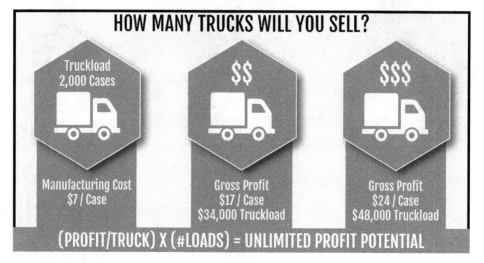

Diagram 1.8 – Truckload Sales Numbers

Now that's perspective! In terms of profit per truckload, the numbers really come into focus, and it's easy to see why profitability is driving this industry to be so hot!

Calculate your own numbers! The example in Diagram 3 uses the example of selling to a distributor to illustrate the minimum sales potential of a $1.99 beverage sold at retail. To calculate your own numbers do the same exercise selling to a retailer and/or directly to the end consumer. Don't forget to calculate your gross profit and gross margin for each!

Why Functional Beverages Are Hot—Supply

We know that commerce is driven by forces of supply and demand. This is the beauty part of New Age and Functional Beverages. Drinks are consumable products. The supply is always being diminished and in need of replenishment.

Unlike one-time buys like DVD's, magazines, and other consumer products, a consumer will buy an energy drink or Tea or a new fancy soda every day if you create in him or her a desire for that product. Let's take a look at this math:

First, let's assume you have a few thousand loyal customers drinking your drink in your city on a daily basis. Let's even be conservative and say 2,000 people buy your drink each day. And we'll only include weekdays; say it's a workday thing and they're drinking your product mid-day Monday through Friday, so say about 20 drinks each month. These consumers are paying an average of $2 per drink (and again, $2 for some drinks will be a conservative figure) at retail.

- o 2,000 drinkers/day
- o x 20 days/month
- o = 40,000 drinks/month
- o 40,000 drinks x $2 each
- o = $80,000/month in retail sales

Profit Potential for Your City

Diagram 1.9 – Profit Potential per City

If we figure the cost of production to be about .29 per bottle, then the gross profit margin on these drinks sales equals out to about $68,400. There will also be other costs such as promotional costs, marketing, overhead, and sales incentives, but as you can see with just a couple of thousand loyal customers you can make some very big money with your business.

Putting up numbers like these, it's easy to see how the promise of continual supply can make this a very hot business to be in for you as a drink developer.

Make sure you take these formulas and style of research and add it to your business plan. If you can realistically show how many consumer you'll convert as daily customers you'll end up with an incredible looking business plan. Add the number of stores that will cater to your new found consumers alongside a retention plan and wow, you're a beverage marketing genius.

Why functional Beverages Are Hot—Demand

It goes without saying that profitability and supply are moot points if there is no market for the product. But this isn't the case at all for new age and functional drinks—the demand for the category is very high. Not only do people want these drinks, they want *new* drinks that can do even more. That leaves a lot of opportunity out there for innovative drink developers.

Unlike other drinks, new age beverages are not just about refreshment; they are about lifestyle and living well. People want these drinks to serve a higher function, to make their lives easier, and to make them look better. As the industry progresses, consumers want drinks that can *do more*. They want not just good tasting drinks, but *functional* drinks. Buyers want drinks that

- Help them meet their health needs
- Fulfill daily dietary and supplement requirements (as is the case with the popular vitamin waters)
- Calm them
- Hydrate them
- Energize them
- Help them focus
- Sexually enhance them
- Enhance memory

Almost any benefit that you can think of is an angle for an energy drink and a potential marketing point. And not least of these benefits are the perception of the drinker—that is, the ability of the drink to make the consumer look better; the function of the drink as a status symbol of sorts. It's what we call the *Starbucks Effect*. What does that mean?

The Starbucks Effect is what people look for in a product that makes them look good; it's similar to people paying top dollars for top brands of mobile phones, PDA's, iPods, and other functional fashion accessories. It doesn't even always matter if the product is really the best and best for them, only that it is fashionable. They want the drink that everyone else is drinking; the one the celebrities carry around; the one their favorite players and idols are drinking—all so they can be 'just like Mike'.

Just like with coffee, consumers could buy their beverages anywhere—McDonald's, 7-Eleven, the corner store—but it wouldn't be *Starbucks* coffee, so it wouldn't be fashionable. When people identify status with your product, you have a drink they will go out of their way to pay outrageous prices for, all because Brad and Angelina drink it or give it to their kids. So be like Starbucks, be like Apple, be fashionable!

The difference with energy drinks and other functional beverages is that unlike products like cell phones and music players, people drink every day. To maintain that benefit—whether the benefit of health, well-being, or status—they need to replenish their supply every day, and that only serves to make the industry hotter and hotter by the day.

These factors—profit, supply, and most of all demand—are what is making new age drinks the hot business to be engaging in. This is why you need to be in the business of producing and supplying this hot and growing market.

Chapter 7

....

Types of Products

What are New Age Beverages and Functional Beverages?

Functional beverages are easy to describe. They have a function, such as energy, relaxation, memory, focus, vitamins, wellness, or any other function. It typically includes energy drinks, energy shots, teas, sports drinks, coffees, and others.

The term "New Age Beverage" is a more traditional term and it can include functional beverages but it can also include any non-traditional beverage or packaging. Anything that is of a new invention or presentation. And where before it was just for non-alcoholic, not it can include alcoholic beverages such as flavored tequila or a new triple distilled homemade cherry vodka. Water, for example, would fit in the new age beverage category but not necessarily in the functional category.

Let's pick on some sub-categories and stretch them out to better understand what they do in the marketplace Let's explore these:

- Water
- Energy drinks and shots
- Enhanced drinks
- Enhanced waters
- New sodas

Water

Water started out very simply as just better quality and more convenient water bottled to meet the needs of consumers on the go and those with access only to poor tasting or poor quality tap water. In Europe bottled water was very popular for many years, not just with Federelle, Perriei or Pelegrino, but with many different brands. I lived in Germany fifteen years ago and I remember bottled water was delivered to homes in one litter glass bottles both flat and carbonated. Al my German friends drank their daily intake of water this way.

Taken as a group, bottled waters are the biggest rival to CSD's, and key industry experts believe the overall water category has what it takes to take that top spot from sodas. As the chairman and CEO of Beverage Marketing Corporation, Michael Bellas, points out, the water category has grown so big it is now starting to splinter into sub-categories; but add those sub-categories back together and you have one huge competitive force in the beverage industry. As he says, with the continued growth of the various water types that are out there, it's only a "matter of time" before sodas are overtaken.
(6)

What does this mega-group look like?

Well, first we have your run-of-the-mill waters—
- Still water
- Spring water
- Sparkling water
- Naturally carbonated water

These waters are classified in a variety of manners, and can come from a variety of sources, including:
- Artesian wells
- Underground streams
- Regular tap

- Glaciers
- Others

A whole list of other options is used to differentiate waters even more, and these unique characteristics are important for marketing and pricing purposes. Examples of the differentiating characteristics are:

- Age of source
- pH level
- Source elevation
- Mineral content
- Bottle material
- Bottle shape
- Cap
- Other marketing distinctions

This mega-water category also includes enhanced waters and flavored waters, but given the nature of the future of these waters we will separate them out and talk about them on their own.

Enhanced Drinks & Waters

Industry reports indicate that the enhanced drinks and flavored water segment of the beverage industry is priming itself for a run at the big-timers. The segment remains a smaller subsection of waters, but enhanced drinks and flavored waters are outperforming their counterparts in the bottled water category.

So what are these cousins to the bottled-water classic that promises to surpass their near relative?

The enhanced drinks and waters segment encompasses a variety of new age products. Some of the common forms of these drinks are:

- Isotonic
- Vitamin enhanced
- Herbal
- Natural
- Organic versions of the same

Producers strive to differentiate these products for consumers by container and design, as well as the quality of vitamins and enhancers used in drink production.

The most successful and "hotter" enhancers for enhanced drinks and waters today are those that are clearly functional; that is to say, the hot enhancers serve a very specific purpose in order to solve problems for drinkers or address health and lifestyle concerns in an effort to appeal to consumers. For example, fruits like pomegranate and acai berries are high in antioxidants—one of today's most touted cancer-prevention and detoxifying agents. Even existing successful drink brands are coming out with new variations that now include "functional" and "fashionable" ingredients so that they can compete with the "do-more" products on the market.

This trend towards increased functionality—getting more from your beverage of choice (or choosing something new that can do more)—is what is driving the NAB market; and when you add that functionality to the already perceived health benefits of waters, you have created an unstoppable force in this more health-conscious world.

Energy Drinks and Shots

There is less to say about energy drinks and energy shots as a product type, but nevertheless this category is a very important product category in functionalbeverages.

When we first wrote the first edition of this book Energy Drinks were the number one category, growing up to 75% per year on the 17 oz cans. The category continued to grow rapidly but not the way we thought. We all thought many different energy drinks would stay in the marketplace representing the diverse tastes and stiles of their consumers. This was not the case. The category consolidated and Monster, Rockstar and Red-Bull stayed on top without flinching. Not even Coke and Pepsi products could kick them out of their pedestals. Now we see Coke distributing Monster Energy and Pepsi picking up Rockstar. All of the other energy drinks have insignificant sales in comparison to these three giants.

Energy Shots was another big surprise. The category opened up at a price point higher than energy drinks for a 2 once shot selling at an official $2.99, although I've see it in Orange County and other high end gas stations for as much as $4.99. Here to the category surprise everyone. 5 Hour Energy Drink sells more than $1 billion in retail sales according to Forbes magazine with no second place competitor coming even close to touching them.

Many of you are familiar with energy drinks; many of us are familiar with them as the pioneers of the functional beverage industry. Energy drinks were, for many people, the first drink to lend functionality and refreshment—the first drinks with a clear purpose. It is this purpose that spurred their vast popularity, despite the fact that a great many energy drinks don't even really taste good. The benefits energy drinks provide often surpass their palatability.

Most energy drinks and shots on the market today are something with perhaps slight carbonation, a few beneficial-sounding ingredients, and something to wake you up—usually large amounts of caffeine. These drinks do not have the level of complexity of enhanced waters and specialty waters, but there are endless options within this category. The successful new energy drinks and all new diversifications will capitalize on those options to create a better tasting and better functioning energy drink for tomorrow. Perhaps they will find healthier and more natural energy-boosters than caffeine; perhaps they will be much improved in taste (probably they will have to be); perhaps they'll reach beyond the work-out set into the hands of office workers and homemakers struggling to make it through the day…as we said, endless possibilities.

We can also deduce from the current lifestyle of Americans, Europeans, and the growing market in Asia and Latin America that the need and desire for better energy will not go away. Life is as harried and chaotic as ever, and people will continue to reach for anything that will help them get through their day; all the better if it tastes good and they believe it to be good for them or a nice fashion accessory, too.

What should you do in this category? Let me tell you first what you should not do, or what others did and failed. Lessons learned and all that jazz. If you'll enter this category focus on Unique Selling Proposition (USP) and Unique Value Proposition (USV). Now you have to identify what counts as a USP and USV and what does not. Yes, you need good taste, but it's not a USP or USV. Don't focus just on packaging unless you have something with intellectual property in your formula. Such as a new substitute for caffeine that works better and only you can use under exclusivity. Your labels will not be your differentiator, or even the size of your beverage.

Now that you know what over five hundred energy drink entrepreneurs did wrong. What you should do? As we said, focus on developing a great USP and USV. One that can carve a niche not with main street consumers, but with niche consumers. The other large piece of advice I would extend is don't go head to head with the billion dollar competitors in their home turf. What's their home turf? Bars, restaurants, hotels, convenience stores, supermarkets and pharmacy. What? You say? That's exactly the places you wanted to sell? Yes I know, you and every other entrepreneur coming into the business. That's precisely the point. You have to find new and alternative channels of distribution. They can be niche, off shore, a brand new target audience, or an entirely different channel, such as direct sales, MLM, mail order, gyms, universities, you add to the list.

For example, the gym that I attend sells local products and this includes local beverages. They sell water from local companies in San Diego and alternative Energy Drinks. I asked them how many energy drinks they sell to share it in the book. Turns out they sell one case per day. That's 24 cans per day. A start-up energy drink might sell one or two cases per month in a local 7-Eleven, so one case per day is incredible. Instead of you selling to 20 stores you just sell to one gym. If you open ten gyms, you're already selling up to three pallets. That's now what you would expect from a normal account. Why not focus on this niche instead of spending up to $1,000 dollars to open a single convenience store? You could also make a deal with a chain of gyms and open 30, 40 50 or 500 gyms, giving them special promotions, sampling, and more. This is not just thinking outside the box or coloring outside the lines, this is changing the game completely, or playing a different game, with your rules, and your home court advantage. As we said before, don't play in their court, they have billions of dollars to compete, you don't.

New Sodas

As sales of carbonated beverages continue to slip after a first-ever drop in sales back in 2005, CSD (Carbonated Soft Drink) producers look for new ways to compete in the more health-conscious consumer marketplace. What they've come up with is a variety of carbonated beverages reminiscent of their roots, but with something more to offer buyers.

And they're offering about everything under the sun. Today, there is a soda for everyone from the extreme sports fan seeking the thrill of the rush to the classy and more sophisticated drinker that prefers a 'healthier' caffeine-free, sugar-free drink in a slim and sexy 10 ounce can.

To meet this new demand for better functioning beverages, soda producers—both old and new—are enhancing their sodas with vitamins and minerals, cutting calories, changing their names to more consumer-friendly monikers like "sparkling beverage," and doing things like adding a dash of juice to naturalize their drinks.

Although sales of CSD's have seen little to no growth (and even negative growth), there is still a place in the beverage industry for sodas; to date, that place stands at around $70 million per year in sales, but that number is likely to change as New Age Beverages further impose their will, and the face of the new sodas will continue to metamorphosize as well. And lest you think that current soda producers are the only ones who can tap the new soda market, think again. In some ways, they've lost face as the "unhealthy" beverage alternative and people seem ready to accept new sodas and new soda producers as a better solution to soda and a happy medium between CSD's and new age drink products.

What can you do to compete in this category?

This is a widely ignored category by entrepreneurs with many possibilities. Just go to your local natural food store to see what soda's they sell and their presentation, usually glass bottles. Think of alternatives methods of distribution like small restaurants or Deli's. Now devise a strategy to penetrate that or other alternative markets with your new product. As always, when developing a product start with your sales strategy, not just how to develop a cucumber sparkling water or a berry-berry so strawberry soda. I've seen many new sodas pop up in the market in the last few year. Some of them sell for as much as $1.99 per bottle and they are sold in four-packs. That's a lot of money for sodas, but they're selling according to the store managers.

The CSD USA retail market sold $76 billion US dollars in 2013 According to Beverage Digest. Down from previous year. This is a very large pie, but remember you're not competing face to face with Coke or Pepsi, you want to find new markets, new consumers, new channels of distribution.

Chapter 8

....

More than Sales:

Business Valuations

The story behind the sale of the most famous beverage companies in the USA, and some that you've never heard about that took their company to the bank.

The sales figure for new age beverages are impressive to be sure; but making money in the beverage business is not just about how many bottles or cans you can sell—it's also about building a valuable business that can, if you so choose, be sold at an extremely handsome profit. Lest you think that we're throwing pie-in-the-sky promises at you, let's take a look at some examples of new age drink brands that started small and made it big. In this chapter we'll highlight some amazing stories of brands that started out as small, independently owned companies and within a few years made millions— that's right million*s,* with an 's'; as in, several million dollars made from the sale of a drink line. Actually, our first story is about a company that made *billions*.

Vitamin Water

Energy Brands Inc., more commonly known as Glacéau, makers of VitaminWater, Smart Water, and Fruit Water, is one of the biggest success stories in the beverage industry.

The company, based out of Whitestone, New York, built a very successful beverage company; and more importantly, a very successful beverage *category* with their "lifestyle" VitaminWater. What is most amazing about this sale is that Glacéau was formed in 1996 and just a little over ten years later, in 2007, it was sold to the Coca Cola Company for billions—$4.1 billion in cash and stocks to be exact.

Coke's President and Chief Operating Officer, Muhtar Kent, gave due credit to the pioneering company, saying, "Glacéau management has been very successful in putting the enhanced water category on the map."[8]

Before the sale, the company maintained its image and grew its distribution through old-fashioned grass-roots marketing. Glacéau relied on independent distributors to carry the product to convenience store and grocery retailers across the U.S. The visionaries of the company used innovative packaging in line with today's market and secured a number of celebrity endorsements as part of their overall marketing strategy. The company so proved their abilities that Bikof and a few other key Glacéau executives will remain on board for a few years to ensure that the company maintains the same passionate— and successful—way of doing business.

Glacéau was an attractive acquisition for Coke because it successfully positioned itself in the enhanced water and energy drink categories, two categories that are credited with making up a significant portion of the beverage industry's growth in North America.

The rest of the stories are mostly measured in millions, not billions, but still the values and sales prices of these businesses are staggering when you consider their roots and their tender age.

Fuze

The growing success of Fuze Beverage LLC first became talk in investment circles in 2004 when Castanea Partners, a Boston-based private investment firm managing a $75 million investment fund, invested in the company. This added not only significant operating cash to the business but also valuable operating experience from the investor that also owned one of the largest independent bottlers of Pepsi in the 1980's. But that was just the beginning of Fuze's success.

Fuze Beverage was formally founded in 2001, after having gotten its start in the basement of co-founder Lance Collins. In the beginning it was just Lance and three others, each with something to offer in the way of business, marketing, and packaging. The idea behind Fuze was to create drinks and teas that really were healthy and beneficial, embarking on lines aimed to "slenderize," "vitalize," "refresh," and do more.

Well before its tenth birthday, Fuze sold to Coke as well, this time for an estimated $250 million; two hundred fifty million dollars for a company that started in a guy's basement in California, and the sale of a company that was only six years in the making.

SoBe

SoBe, which stands for South Beach Beverages, may sound like it was started in the calm, quiet, and relaxation of a warm coastal California beach, but it was actually started in Norwalk, Connecticut. Four partners, including John Bello and Tom Schwalm, all interested in health and fitness and all with the mission of creating healthier and more functional drinks, started SoBe in 1996 with the introduction of their SoBe Black Tea 3G; the 3 G's stood for Ginseng, Gingko, and Guarana. The first tea was so successful that they expanded the line to include more teas and energy drinks; today the SoBe line includes Life Water, too.

Like others, SoBe's success caught the attention of the big beverage companies looking for a way to expand into the hot NAB market and compete against their rivals. In 2000, just four years after its founding, SoBe sold to Pepsi for approximately $370 million.

Fiji

Fiji Water got its start simply enough. The owner of a club in Fiji noted that guests were often lugging in their own bottled water and went off in search of a local source to supply his club with good-tasting drinking water. What he found was a natural water source deep within the island that he began to bottle and sell as "untouched by man;" he marketed his water as superior in purity and excellence and soon rose to be the second leading supporter of imported bottled water in the United States. Ironically, what started as a way to supply his guests with better tasting local water turned out to be a huge beverage export business, and most of the water bottled from the source is now exported instead.

Fiji Water expanded its line and sold in 2004 to Roll International, owners of Teleflora and Pom Wonderful pomegranate juice. Industry sources say the sales price for this simple water bottling company was $63 million.

Snapple

In many ways Snapple was one of the first new age beverage brands. The company is not young, though; it actually was started in the 1940's, but really took off in the 1970's. Snapple was also one of the first big-dollar NAB purchases, selling to Quaker Oats for $1.7 billion in 1994. Quaker failed at managing the established brand properly and they re-sold the diminished brand to Cadbury for $300 million in 2000. The resale at a loss to Quaker, and the willingness of Cadbury to pay hundreds of millions for a struggling new age drink can be taken as proof that the promise of a successful NAB is still a high value for a company with vision.

Perspective on Beverage Valuations

It's important to include these examples so that readers understand the true potential of their new age drinks line. While the promise of owning a profitable NAB is a great reason to get into the industry, the potential of selling that well-established brand is equally encouraging.

Having this perspective is important if you are to understand how you will profit from your NAB business. There is a perception by many drink developers that they will be selling hundreds of millions of dollars worth of their drinks; that is not realistic. The biggest new age beverages are selling about $200 million per year, perhaps a little more for Red Bull. The others are not as close. Still, these businesses are valued between $100 million and $500 million, sometimes more. When you compare the figures you see that the sale price of the business really has no relevance to the amount of product that was actually selling. It's more related to the potential of a brand that has proven itself and what the buyer thinks they can accomplish by purchasing the NAB.

Something else to consider is that there is a great potential for investment in this business, as exemplified in the story of Fuze. Keep in mind that in almost all of these cases the drinks were started based on ideas—not necessarily on access to funds; if you have a good idea *and a solid business plan* for a promising new age beverage, there are investors that are more than willing to invest in it. We get inquiries from investors all the time looking to cash in on the NAB craze while the market is still hot. They're just looking for someone like you who can develop the drink on their behalf. The caveat is that smart investors don't throw their money at ideas; they put their money into planned product development. That's all the more reason you need this book, so that you can prove to investors you are well-versed in drink development, and you know how to succeed where so many others have failed.

In the end, for you, as a new age drink developer evaluating the potential for profit in this market, the outlook is very good; the potential to profit from both product sales and the sale of a product line creates even larger opportunities, and so business valuation is yet another factor that you need to consider along the way.

Coca-Cola and start-ups

Coke is not only buying and investing in large companies and like the $2.15 billion investment into Monster Energy Drink in 2015 according to a Coke's press release or the 17% acquisition of Green Mountain Coffee for $2 billion according to the Wall Street Journal article dated December 7, 2015. Coke is also buying smaller companies and investing in new company.

Coca-Cola has been the most active in non-alcoholic beverage investments and acquisitions. They started a new division called Venturing and Emerging Brands or VEB. This is their description on their LinkedIn group:

> *"We were created with an ambitious purpose: to find and develop the next generation of brands with billion-dollar potential. We welcome entrepreneurs and other professionals to join our group!"*

Anyone can join VEB's LinkedIn group. I encourage you to join this discussion group allowing you to interact with VEB and other entrepreneurs.

VEB currently owns and manages brands such as Honest Tea, Hubert's lemonade and Zico coconut water. The company invests in upcoming companies of all sizes and partners with investment groups to reach more investments. Their website is a reach source of information on what they're investing in at any time.

The VEB portfolio is filled with incredible beverage success stories. Many from entrepreneurs that started with no money, no product, and no idea of what they were doing. They managed to work and grew their company to the point Coke was interested in investing and latter in buying the company.

PART TWO

DEVELOPING AND
LAUNCHING YOUR DRINKS

Chapter 9

....

Everything You Need to
Develop & Launch Your Drinks

Let's go through the steps a new entrepreneur or executive takes when first deciding to go into the beverage industry. This will help you see what the majority of people do and give you new tools in deciding how to approach your own path in beverage development.

"I've spent $250,000 and an entire year trying to develop my beverage and I'm now discouraged and out of money" This is a typical call any day of the week at the office. To hear some of the stories from clients you would think beverage development is like rocket science. It's really not. It's actually much harder than rocket science... nop, just kidding.

Beverage Development is very easy, launching a beverage is not so easy; that's why you have to start with your launching idea, in other words, with your business model. Beverage development is based on project management best practices and launching a beverage is based on market timing, distribution acceptance, consumer interactions, your marketing budget, management team and a bit of luck.

The Good News –You'll learn those beverage development business best practices, we call the entire process "Reverse Engineering" or start at the end, end in the beginning.

Beverage development is the next part of the book. What you'll learn here is applicable to each and every one of you interested in launching a new age beverage, regardless of your background and entry into this field. It doesn't matter if you are an existing beverage company looking to cross over into the energy drink, functional and new age beverage market to exploit this new beverage boom, if you are a distributor wanting to produce and distribute your own label, if you are an investor searching for worthwhile Beverage start-ups to make money with, or if you are an entrepreneur with a great product concept; whoever you are, all you need to know to develop and launch your new age drink starts here.

A Formula for Success for All Drinks

All types of drinks follow the same basic process for development up until the launch. This is the process we will outline here. This process is fundamental to success with new beverages, as it is with all other types of beverages including alcoholic and non-alcoholic drinks. It's a proven process because it is the same process that has been used to launch every *successful* drink product on the mass market today (whether or not the developer realized what he or she was doing). We've used this process for our own beverages as well as for clients.

Yes, there are particularities in every beverage project and special ingredients, packaging or artwork that will go into your drink, but the best practices, the process, the formula is the same for all companies and all drinks. What happens when you deviate from this plan? You start getting into problems. You spend too long on artwork, you realize your artwork was already trademarked, you're bottle does not fit on the right refrigerator, or the most common, you spend too much time and too much money.

The Ins and Outs of the Industry from Production and Beyond

There are some basic points you need to know before you jump into a beverage development. These include:

1. Target market
2. Research
3. Formulation & Ingredients
4. Warehouse &Transportation
5. Distribution Channels
6. Consumer Communication

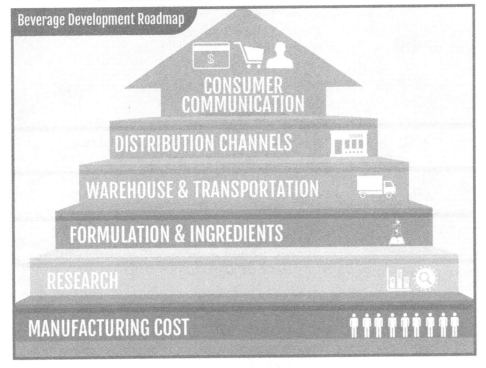

Diagram 2.1 – Beverage Development Roadmap

You'll see Target Market in many of these chapters. No, it's not because we forgot we mentioned it before, it's because it's the most important think in beverage development. Actually it's the most important thing in sales, in distribution, in marketing and in the book. Target market, or your target consumer is the entire basis of Reverse Engineering Beverage Development because you start with your consumer and move backwards through the entire beverage development process.

Beginning at the End—Reverse Engineering

Ultimately the success of your new age drink will rely on the end result. No, I don't mean the taste, I mean the sales, or consumer acceptance. This is why this is the most important part of your entire beverage development process, this is the process you'll use when bringing your idea to life.

Yes, costs are important, so is artwork and formula and all the other components that will go into producing your beverage, but without the process, without your project management having the costs and co-packer is just information on a page, what project managers call line items or deliverables, now it's time to learn how to convert it all into your beverage. For all of this to work we'll start at the end – you guessed it, we'll start with your consumer.

Why not start at the beginning?

Only by starting at the end, by having a clear vision of your product, your market, and your goals, can you know what type of product, marketing, and sales and distribution lines are right for your product; only this way can you know how to meet your customers' needs. At the risk of repeating ourselves, if there is one mistake we see made in this business time and again it is the mistake of developing your product first, and thinking about who will buy it and where second. When you do this you run a very big risk of having an excellent product that is improperly packaged and miserably marketed; one that never gets beyond the discount dollar store shelves.

These are the correct steps for beverage development:
1. Find your perfect consumer
2. Where do they buy? = Your Retailer
3. Who delivers to that channel = Your Distributor
4. Channel Pricing = Price to distributor, retailer, consumer
5. Concept = USP and USV
6. Artwork = labels, look and feel, colors
7. Package = Bottle, can, other
8. Formulation = Color, taste and function
9. Production = Now you are ready

This is how entrepreneurs usually develop beverages:
1. Idea
2. Google searches
3. Formulation
4. Artwork
5. Production
6. Pricing

You'll notice this last process is lacking items that relate to search and marketing, such as retail, distributor, and other information, many entrepreneurs realize this only after they have product in the ware house and notice retailers and distributors don't take the product, or they miscalculated their costs of production and spent to much money in relation to what retailers would pay for their product. All of this is part of your research.

Channel pricing, retailers, distribution, and finding your consumer are integral parts of your research, so is speaking with as many distributors, retailers and consumers as possible about your idea before spending a dime. You might discover they already tried your idea and it didn't work.

In finding your perfect consumers write down who they are, their age, where do they shop, how much money they make, do they have a family? Do they travel? Do they exercise? Find out everything about them. If you don't know everything about them try imagining it as if you're creating a character. This information will allow you to start establishing an emotional relationship with your consumer, and the wholly grail of marketing. It will also tell you where your consumer buys, is it at a 7-Eleven or at a supermarket, do they go out to bars or do they only eat at restaurants, how much they will spend, and much more.

Start first by determining who this product is going to be for. Once we know who is going to buy your drink we can work on the overall concept. This in turn helps us determine very practical matters like flavoring and product packaging.

After we know what type of product you will be producing and in what types of packaging, we can look towards finding a bottler capable of mixing and filling your drink given the specifications of your beverage. As you'll learn, there is more to this part of the process than meets the eye, because not all bottlers are the same, and not all have the same capabilities for handling the same types of products, bottling supplies, and processes.

Finally, once we have all of this information firmly under hand, we can start talking about distribution and sales in more depth. We'll need to develop some of this as we go, at least in basic terms, in order to properly develop your drink, and then we will finalize the deal after by showing you how to do the real work involved with marketing, distributing, and selling.

Case Study Example: Uni:Te

Here is a good case study to put it all together. We just finished developed Uni:Te for a new beverage entrepreneur. Larry Gilmore, the CEO had no previous beverage experience.

Here is the tale of the tape:
Name: Uni:Te
Product: Ready to drink and brewed tea (2 products)
Special Ingredients: Seeds of the date fruitIntellectual
Property: Production process

When Larry first called us he wanted to sell to small ethnic stores around the country by creating specialty beverages for each niche. In theory this is a fantastic idea. In practice it's a nightmare; not only for him but for us, as we had to handle sales and distribution. It's a nightmare because each niche has a different sales and distribution channel, not to mention an entirely different customer base. This means each time he comes up with a new beverage we need to do all the work from scratch.

For example, the first product was meant for the Hispanic population, specifically the Mexican-American niche. This means we need to look for Mexican supermarkets around the USA as well as the distributors serving these accounts. If Larry launches an Asian product next time we'll can't use the same supermarkets or the same distributors. That's a big problem and it will take a lot of money and time to target all those different niches.

Yes, that's a big problem, but it wasn't the biggest problem. The first thing we needed to do is convince Larry not to develop his Date Tea for the Mexican-American target market. It wasn't easy. The reason we needed to change the target market is easy, Dates don't come from Mexico! It's not a Mexican tradition and consumers in Mexican supermarkets in the USA will not pay the premium price commanded by this specialty product. It is a great product but the consumer is not the Mexican-American consumer and the target market is the Natural Channel, not the "Mexican" channel.

What happens now?

Uni:Te avoided several huge mistakes from the start and saved thousands of dollars in development and production of the wrong beverage plus the time and money to sell the product. In my estimates they saved around $85,000 just by making the right decision.

Uni:Te was developed for the Natural Channel where the market is the affluent consumer that is willing to try new, natural products and pay a premium for this product.

In this case my team worked on the entire project as full product managers including research, strategy, formulation, artwork, photography, events, project management, pricing structure, mentoring and consulting.

After this was done the team developed point of sale material, marketing material, website, and everything necessary to sell to consumers, retailers and distributors.

How does a beverage development process work?

For this let's dip into our beverage development best practices. We've developed these over 11 years of product development with more than 1,000 different projects with production in the USA, China, Mexico and Europe.

Here are the steps we used for the development of Uni:Te:

1. Initial Consultation by Phone
2. Strategy Session with Client in Person
3. Project Manager Assignment
4. Concept Consultation with Client

5. Retail and Wholesale Research
6. Internal Product Meetings
7. Concept Development
8. Concept Approval
9. Face-to-Face Meeting
10. Artwork Development
11. Package Development
12. Formulation Testing
13. Samples of Formulation
14. Approval of Formulation
15. Approval of Package and Artwork
16. Production
17. Sales and Marketing Collateral
18. Mentoring in Person

At the end we developed a ready to drink product in a bottle and a bagged product that you brew at home.

Do you have a case study you would like to share? Go to BuildYourBeverageEmpire.com and send it to us. We'll share it on a podcast or webinar. It will get you free promotion!

In the next chapter you will discover how much it will all cost. How much money you need to develop, formulate, and produce your best-selling beverage.

Chapter 10

....

Know Your Costs

How much money does it take?

That is the bottom line, isn't it? If you are interested in the beverage industry as a business or as an investment opportunity it may be the only line that matters to you. If you are developing your drink as an entrepreneur, the figure on the bottom line will be just as important in the product development phase, because what you can afford is determined by the cost, yes? If you're an investor placing your trust in the entrepreneur you need to know how much money to give them to get started with proof of concept, development and production.

The hard part is in finding the answer to this question. There is no real way for us to give you a hard and fast figure because there are so many possibilities and combinations within the industry and between different concept drinks. What you'll get is a guide that will give you some ideas and the guidance to research your own costs more accurately.

From this chapter you will get a sort of worksheet, a manual that you can use to plug in the costs you know now and those that you can research so that you can determine the feasibility of your concept as is right now, and as you develop your drink further. To know your exact cost we would need to know at least the basics about your concept. Things like artwork ideas, production minimums for your package, co-packing costs for your category and the ingredients that go into your product. If you want cans, you have to pay a higher minimum that if you want bottles. If want a custom bottle that's more money for the mold and the bottle design and specifications. This is why it's important to research your beverage before investing anything.

Why Research Costing Now?

The short answer to this question is that you have to research your costing right now, at the beginning, to make sure you can afford the production of your drink. But this step has a larger importance, and that is to establish that there is in fact enough of a margin, or that you can create enough of a profit-margin with sales to make the drink profitable. That also means knowing what your consumer will pay for the product. If you're research is incorrect you can have a wonderful product that your target consumer can't afford.

We get a lot of people calling us, often times distributors and small drink distributors, telling us that they've purchased x amount of cases of a new drink that they've been trying to sell and profit from with little luck. Many times we have to break the bad news to these people and tell them that there's not enough margin in the product—they either bought it too high or they produced it themselves at too high a cost for what the market can support.

A typical phone call is where someone produced a couple of pallets of a beverage or energy drink at $20 or $25 per case of 24 - 8 ounce drinks instead of the $7 to $12 for a case of 24 - 16 ounce cans that they should have and they couldn't sell the drinks to distributors—because the distributors know that the wholesale cost is too high and they won't be able to profit off it; they'd lose out by selling this drink at a very low profit margin and lose the sales of other, higher-profiting drinks. There are two reasons why we get these types of calls:

The entrepreneur didn't research their costs ahead of time
Someone took advantage of them

Sometimes it's both—how would you know when someone is
taking advantage of you if you don't know the accurate costs
of producing an energy drink or new age beverage?

Having vision is helpful in this business, but doing your
research is absolutely imperative. You absolutely must do the
market research, market analysis, and cost analysis, and you
absolutely must learn about the beverage industry, just like
you are doing now.

Before jumping into minute detail on costing let's do a CEO's
view of costing. We can divide the major categories into
Development and Sales. Development is everything up to
production. It does not include warehousing or transportation,
sales, printing of materials used for sales, travel, trade shows
or anything else that falls into sales. It only includes the
process of beverage development from your idea to the final
product in production or co-packing.

You then divide the Development phase into clear and simple
points that you can budget and schedule using a timeline and
goals for your deliverables. Here is how it will look:

- Concept Development
- Legal
- Formulation
- Small Run & Large Run Production

Using these four steps as your guideline will keep you out of
trouble, out of spending too much money and out spending
money on marketing, public relations or other things before
you have your product ready.

ITEM	Do it Yourself	Be Worried	Target Cost
Concept Development	$15,000	Under $10,000	$25,000 to $50,000
Legal	DON'T	DON'T	$3,500
Formulation	DON'T	Under $5,000	$5,000 to $10,000
Small Run Production	DON'T	More than $25 / case	$15 to $22 / case
Normal Production	DON'T	More than $12	$9 to $12 / case

Diagram 2.2 – Beverage Development Costs

The Beverage Development Costs graph gives you an overview of what your costs should for the major cost categories. Legal costs refer only to costs associated to the development of the beverage, such as label review, and not any other legal advice, intellectual property or creation of your corporation or LLC.

Beverage Operational Costs
After product comes out of the production line you have other costs associated with operating your business. These include things like warehousing, sales, or marketing. Here is an overview of costs you can include in your research.

- Warehousing
- Transportation
- Marketing

Doing the Research

Doing your research is imperative. It bears repeating. Research is important for costing but also for everything related to your product. If you don't have the right research you will not know if your product has a place in the marketplace. Going to a store to look at the shelves and looking on the internet is the research that I'm talking about. Yes, it's a good start but it will only tell you what everyone knows. You want to know what nobody else knows.

But what do we mean by research? By research we mean a variety of things; research may be:

- The most common sense of the word where you start reading and investigating through informational resources—such as this book
- Evaluating statistics
- Field research at counters and convenience stores
  - o Actually looking on store shelves
  - o Pay attention to marketing
  - o Find similar products and evaluate their sales
  - o Find the product(s) that are missing that present an open market
- Calls to retailers and distributors
- Face to face conversations with retailers; especially focus on stores in the city where you plan to sell first; ask
  - o Would you consider taking on this product?
  - o How much are you buying product X for?
  - o Who is the distributor for this product?
  - o Get as much information as you can—it's all part of creating your own brand!

To get the most accurate and complete picture, your research should be all of these things. In your research you are looking to answer a few key questions as they apply to your drink concept; you want to find out:

- Is there a place for your product?
- Who is your perfect consumer
- How to get product to your consumer
- How to communicate with your consumer

- Who are your competitors?
- How much are they making?
- How much is the retailer making? The distributor?
- What are freight costs?
- How is this product sold or how will you sell this product? By the truckload? Pallet? Case?

Realize that as you progress through the planning and development of your drink the answers to these types of questions might change; you may find that your drink does not carry a wide enough profit margin as-is, and you may have to make changes. That's okay; in fact, that's the point!

The point is to do the research and make those changes now so that by the time your drink is actually bottled you have a meticulously planned product with a clear plan for distribution, sales, and marketing.

The most important research

The most important type of research will not be the one that comes from your local convenience store or supermarket. It will be from speaking with distributors and buyers at retail accounts. Yes, your research comes from conversations. My team currently calls up to 2,000 buyers or decision makers every single month to tell them about new products. During those calls they ask these buyers about what their looking for, buying trends, what works and what doesn't work in the stores.

I'm not suggesting you call 2,000 people per month, but you should at least call 10 to 20 people and get some insight from them.

What's wrong with search engine research? Nothing is wrong with doing research on the internet, the problem is it will not give you the right information, same with retail stores. It will only tell you what is already in the marketplace and what's successful, not what failed.

Let's paint a picture. You have an idea for a special type of beverage; let's say it's Orange Tea in a ready to drink 16 ounce bottle. You search online for Orange Tea and you see there is no competition. You're happy! You visit the stores and you see there is no Orange Tea in the refrigerators or on the shelves. You're convinced, you'll be first to market with a brewed tea packed with vitamin C form oranges but low in sugar as a great substitute to orange juice. You now invest in development and production and a few months later and after more than $100,000 you have product in the warehouse.

It's time to sell your Orange Tea. You call some beverage distributors, you go to a trade show and meet with the buyers from a convenience store and a supermarket that can buy for up to 10,000 stores. You're very happy. You sit down at your first meeting and the distributor tells you "We tried exacly this product 10 years ago and 5 years ago and 2 years ago, and after 3 failures we're convinced the product is not for us".

You sit with the retailers "That product doesn't work" they say, "We've tried it several times and it didn't sell, call me when you have something else".

Can this really happen? You bet – it happens every single day with new products. Just a few calls to the right decision makers would have told you the traditional retail channels will not buy your product. It doesn't mean it's a bad product, it doesn't mean consumers somewhere will not embrace it. It means you didn't do your homework. You forgot to research the correct channels.

If you would like to do even more targeted research try to sell your product to consumers. You can do this by spending a bit of money in a website with sales capabilities. Test your product by selling it to consumers. If consumers buy your product distributors and retailers will probably take it. If not today then once you grow your customer base.

The Cost of Concept Development

Your Concept is your number one priority as a beverage creator. It's what makes your beverage different, unique, and sellable. It's your idea and the way you'll market your idea. It's the backbone of everything else.

This step will create your artwork, package and the entire look and feel of the product including the color of the beverage itself, the bottle or can that you will use and the entire Consumer Experience.

The most important thing about concept is the Consumer Experience. When you or your designer or project team talks about the brand, the colors, the concept always start with "what will the consumer do" or "what will the consumer feel". This will help you answer questions such as size of the product, color, position in the store and in the shelve, price, marketing, point of sale material and a variety of other things you need to answer before you even start drawing your logo or your bottle. You don't start your concept with a graphic designer; you start it with a consumer.

Concept is where you should spend the majority of your money in and most of your time and effort. Don't spend your time calling co-packers, formulators or ingredient providers. The concept will tell you all you need to know to develop a product that sells, and that's what you want, not a product that just looks good, or tastes good, but one that sells.

Concept development can range from $200 to $100,000 or more. A vitamin company that we worked with got designs for their vitamins for $200 including logo and a bottle rendering how it will look on their bottle. They got this from an internet artwork bidding website and received 5 different concepts. Is that a deal or what? They thought it was great, but when they called a co-packer they realized they could not use it. They still had to pay for the UPC, label legalities, and create the label according to their specifications. At the end they paid $1,000. Wow, that's still a great deal.

Yes, you can pay $1,000 for your label with everything you need, however it will not be a label that you would want to invest your time and money to produce and sell. If you're going to spend another $20,000 to $50,000 in production plus the cost of sales why would you spend $1,000 in the most important part of the process?

Remember, the $1,000 was for a logo and label not for a Concept. A Concept means all research with consumers, distributors and wholesalers was done.

Large companies can spend more than $1 million dollars in concept. They use expensive firms and go through consumer exercises such as focus groups in different parts of the country. They can even test product in niche stores to see the reaction of the consumer. We will not go into these budgets because we want to concentrate our efforts in small and medium size companies that are developing their products.

Spending $25,000 to $50,000 would be acceptable for this phase of the project if you're working with the right team, not a designer or a private label firm that just produces cans or shots with your label.

You can spend less, maybe even $15,000 if you do all the research and concept on your own. By all means do this if you're already in the beverage industry or in product development and have several years of experience in merchandising or marketing. If you don't have this experience you'll need to spend some time getting it, at least two or three years at a director or VP level. However if you're not a veteran of the industry it will be time or money. Spend the money and do it right.

Legal

For legal fees we're only talking about fees related to a normal production of a ready to drink beverage with standard formulation using an FDA approved formulator and co-packer. They already spent some money in legal fees making their facilities compliant.

If you're starting a production plant or have a special ingredient not currently sold in your country this is an entirely different story. Expect to pay $3,500 for label review, FDA review and other legalities related to production. This does not include the formation of your corporation or other legal entity or any type of intellectual property like your trademark or patents. You have to add that to your costs. Before you choose a name and produce one million bottles with that name make sure somebody else doesn't have the trademark. Yes, I've see this happen many times.

Formulation

Formulation used to be free a few years ago. Ingredient houses would create a formula for you and make money from selling you the ingredients. This is not true anymore. The problem is too many people call them and ask for a formula never to product their product again. Now you have to pay for your formulation and in many cases you don't own it. Yes, you heard correct, it comes as a shocker to many people that they pay ingredient houses $5,000 and they don't own the formula. This happens because their cost is higher than $5,000 and they want to make money with the sale of ingredients. If they release your formula you can go and buy your ingredients elsewhere.

Don't worry too much; your formula can probably be duplicated by anyone at any time if you need a formulator to develop it. Your value, the value of your brand is not the formula, if it is you're in big trouble. If you just want to create a product that tastes good, or at least better than your competitor, you'll be out of business before anyone can even taste it. Your real value is in the relationships you can make with the consumer; in the unique distribution channels or in your supply chain.

You don't have to use formula houses to produce your formula, you can do it with independent formulators or laboratories that will give you the formula. You can then take it to a recommended ingredient house and purchase the ingredients from them. Ask the formulator for a list of ingredient suppliers that will supply all the ingredients before you start the project. If you fail to do so you might find yourself re-formulating and paying again for the formula. This happens about thirty percent of the time.

If your formulation is simple $5,000 to $10,000 is very reasonable for a base formula. Make sure it includes shipping costs to you for sampling. It might also include an extra flavor using the same base formula. It will not include an entirely different flavor or ingredient base.

If your formulation is not standard and requires special ingredients or a special process you'll have to pay more, up to $20,000 or more depending on how complex it is. The good news is I only see one or two of this per year. You're probably in the $5,000 to $10,000 price range.

Drink Production Costs

Drink production costs are the expenses incurred from the physical product and packaging. We will go into each of these in more depth in chapters dedicated to them; here, we've compiled a quick list of the primary elements that need to be accounted for as you start determining the costing for your new age beverage.

The easiest way we can explain this is to ask you to think about your end-product. Envision your drink and look at the various components that comprise it. You'll have the:

- Container; usually glass, plastic, or aluminum
- Top; caps, seals, sometimes a second safety or freshness seal, too
- Labeling; not only the type and size of the label, but also design and artwork costs involved with hiring graphics professionals—there are a lot of options here and the cost can run anywhere from a fraction of a cent to several cents per label
- Ingredients and flavors; here the sky is the limit and you will find a great diversity of ingredients and costs, but they will be the cornerstone of your drink

Once your drinks are prepared and bottled they also have to be packed for transport and distribution. You can't just send loose bottles onto a truck. Single bottles need to be packaged into cases, which are boxed or wrapped, and then bundled into pallets ready for shipping via trucks. There is an additional cost here, too, and you'll also need to add up the costs of whatever it is you choose to use (either a cardboard case [box], a tray [a box cut in half] and/or plastic wraps).

Of course, we cannot forget that the bottler is paid for his part, too.

Many people come into this business thinking that they have to set up their own bottling facility; that is not cost-effective for anyone but the big, established drink producers. For your drink you should be outsourcing all production. There are hundreds of thousands of beverage plants throughout the country whose only business is co-packing. A Co-packer is basically a bottling facility that has different lines of products that they produce for others. Each facility is different and handles different types of products, processes, and packaging (for example, glass, plastic, hot-fill, cold-fill, organic, etc.). You contract them and give your product specifications and they do the rest, handing back to you a completed drink product that you now have to manage.

This covers the elemental costs of drink production that will tell you how much it will cost to get your drink produced—to get it made and bottled—but costs do not end here; you're ready now with a drink waiting to go out the doors, but we still have a long way to go.

Small Run and Large Run Production

Don't try to save money by starting with a large production run. Yes, it's much cheaper per case or per can or bottle to produce five or ten truckloads, don't do it. Spend a few dollars more and produce a small run of production, maybe one truckload or even less if permitted. Test that product in stores, with distributors and with consumers. Open a few stores and once you have orders and re-orders ramp-off your production accordingly.

Yes, you guessed it; I've seen companies produce ten thousand cases of 24 cans only to through them away because they expired. I see this up to once per month. Avoiding this is very simple and it's great business. Just test your product first. Production of small runs can cost up to double, or even more, of a normal run, but in dollars it could be the difference between $20,000 and $300,000.

You can pay from $15 to $22 per case of 24 of a regular product without any fancy expensive ingredients in a small run. I produce around 1,000 to 2,000 cases for test purposes before going to a real production run. Normal production runs can go as low as $6 per case with volume if you're a very large company, but for start-ups expect to pay in the range of $9 to $12 per case. When do you know if it's too much? If you're not making at least 50% margin (100% mark-up) you're not at the right retail price or you're paying too much for production.

POS

The costs that come after production costs are what are called Point of Sale, or POS costs. POS is everything you need to communicate effectively and economically with the consumer. This cost are part of your initial investment because it's expected from you, from your brand. Retailers expect to get stickers, posters, and other materials to sell your product in their stores. Distributors expect to get t-shirts, hats, sell sheets and other sales collateral to push your products into retailers, restaurants and bars.

POS costs include all of your

- Sales materials
- Manufacturing costs
- Point of Sale materials (in-store advertising, marketing…things that get products sold off the shelves)
- Cost of transportation from manufacturer to distributor to warehouse
- Warehouse costs
- Sales costs
- Slotting costs
- Other costs such as websites, distributor expenses, incentives, third-party logistics

POS costs encompass a lot and the cost here is very important; neglecting to flesh-out these costs could spell disaster for your drink before you ever get it into a store.

Warehousing

Once your drink is produced at the bottler it cannot stay there. This is often something people do not think about until they get to the point of bottling, and so this is one of the costs that, although very significant indeed, can be easily overlooked. However, your drink will not go straight from the bottler to the distributor or retailer either and so you will have to incur the additional cost of warehousing it. There are a number of costs involved in warehousing that will affect your specific warehousing costs, including

- Material handling
- Equipment
- Employees
- Racks
- Rent
- Space and amount of product [number of pallets]

This again is a cost you will want to outsource, and one that you must account for. (We'll break down the costs and options further in the chapter on Warehousing).

Transportation

How will you get from point A to point B with your product? You'll pay to have it transported.

Transportation costs are very much dependent on how much product is moved and how often. You need to know your transportation costs, but you also have to keep them variable as extra movements and changes in the cost of trucking and transporting can really make transportation costs add up.

The key to accurately researching transportation costs is to really think them through. This does not mean just calculate the cost to move your drink from bottler to warehouse and warehouse to distributor; it also means to include the little costs that are easily overlooked that really add up. It includes thinking through transportation costs down to the mailing of single samples.

Shipping costs for mailings and sample distribution is all part of your transportation cost. It's one thing if you are sending out just a few single samples here and there, but once you start sending samples in quantity—sending three, four, or five cases to each distributor—and using the mail, UPS, FedEx, DHL, etc., it gets very expensive. All of these costs must be considered and included in your business plan.

Sales

Sales costs cover the costs involved in getting your new age beverage into stores and/or selling venues and then sold off the shelves. Sales costs can cover a variety of expenses and will vary depending on the type of sales channels you will be using to sell your products.

Many drink developers think of sales costs as being the costs paid to support or maintain sales representatives who in turn will do the selling for them, but in reality there is more involved. When you are starting out, you may not have a sales representative; otherwise you may have a sales rep assigned to your product through the distributor. In any case, you have to plan to go a step further than the salary or cost of the sales representative. You have to spend money to support that representative by providing sales materials and marketing, and you often have to give the representative an incentive to make him want to sell your product.

Incentives for sales representatives are important, and also often overlooked by new drink developers. They think, 'but isn't it the sales representative's job to sell my product?' It is, but you have to keep in mind that sales reps usually have other products they are selling too, and they will go with the product that makes them [personally] the most money. In other words, if you make it financially beneficial to the sales representative to push your product, you will enjoy more sales. This is often done by offering commissions and incentives for 'X' amount of product sold. What happens if you don't give the sales representative an incentive? Usually it means your drink samples are those left sitting in the trunk of the car while other, more profitable drinks get all the attention.

Besides sales reps and marketing and support materials, sales costs can be other expenses taken in the interest of selling, such as:

- Slotting costs (paying for premium shelf space)
- Websites
- Distributor incentives
- Retailer incentives

Often the costing involved with sales is what can make or break your drink's profitability if not carefully planned for. For instance, incentives can really boost your sales and the effort a sales rep, retailer, or distributor will put into your product, but if you are too generous or have not accurately calculated the profit margin to allow for all incentive costs, there may be no profit left to be made.

Similarly, slotting can be a drink's boon or a bust. Slotting fees vary by chain and can be very reasonable or astronomical in comparison to your profit margin. On the one hand paying slotting fees is one of the fastest ways to get into the massive grocery chains, but on the other they are normally reserved for those with deep pockets, making them sometimes an unreasonable cost that your new drink cannot support (it may be worth noting here that we have never paid a slotting fee, but have launched a number of very profitable drink products!).

There is a time and a place for slotting fees for many drinks, but first you have to be sure the market is worth being in to begin with. People who want to get into this business often think that the big grocers like Wal-Mart or Kroger's are the place to be; there are two problems with this line of thinking:

1. It's too difficult to get into the big stores like Wal-Mart until you've established some sales
2. You need a large amount of cash flow to carry these large vendors' receivables
3. Big stores are not necessarily where you want to be

What developers don't realize is that the big sales for energy drinks and new age beverages are out in the trenches, not at the grocery counter. People buy NAB's primarily at convenience and liquor stores and small corner markets where people are buying on-the-go refreshment or looking for a quick pick-me-up. It's also important to note here that when you do sell big in the small stores, the big stores will come looking for you to provide your product to your now loyal customer base.

Many Hands Make Fine Work

From the beginning you should understand the role that others will play in the development, production, and sale of your energy drink or NAB; although you may feel that your drink is your 'baby' and that you are the one who is best-suited to manage it in all ways, that is not a cost-effective costing strategy. The most cost-effective drink production strategy is one that delegates different aspects of production and outsources to the appropriate facilities and professionals. Throughout the drink development and production process, you will need the help of many outside sources for supplies and production including:

- Flavor house/ingredient house
- Packaging and graphics designers
- Bottle/can/package supplier (this isn't usually your bottler)
- Bottler (who fills the drinks)
- Warehouses
- Distributors
- Sales representatives
- Retailers

Understanding this from the beginning will allow you to perform accurate cost analysis to come up with not only true costs and expectations, but also big money-savings by putting drink production in the hands of professionals who are set up to do the job. In the end, outsourcing and relying on your partner companies will turn dividends much in your favor.

The Final Tally

We've thrown a lot of different costs and variables out at you throughout this chapter, but we probably have still not really answered what you want to know: "How much will it cost me to develop and produce my new age beverage?"

To answer this question, we'll run you through the process of production, utilizing the various outsourcing resources you will be using as you develop your drink.

The ballpark figure that we use for drink production is between $7 and $12 per case for a product case of 24 drinks.

Multiply that times your run size (number of cases in the production run) and you have a ballpark cost for your first run. Most bottling facilities have a minimum run of 5,000 cases. But this only covers the actual production and filling of the product. First you'll need to buy cans or bottles to fill.

One thing we find that people do not know, and so do not plan for, is that they have to buy bottles or cans from one facility or supplier and have it bottled with another. Using cans as an example, in the U.S. there are two major manufacturers of cans. You'll go to them, have them produce and print your can, and you buy 8,000 cases of cans, 24 cans per case (as you might guess, you'll start thinking in terms of cases, not cans, soon enough; the industry deals in terms of cases). Major American can and bottle manufacturers have a minimum order of 8,000 cases of cans. Once those are printed you'll have them trucked ($) to the filler, the bottling company, where the ingredients will already be (either you will have bought them and had them sent or the bottler will have bought them on your behalf; either way the cost is yours).

This is where the first discrepancy in costing comes in. You now have 8,000 cases of cans, but the bottler will only require you to fill 5,000 cases in each run. You need to decide to either fill all 8,000 cases ($) or fill the minimum and store ($) the other 3,000 cases for the next time. This discrepancy may not seem logical to you, but from a supply and production perspective it does make sense; 8,000 cases is one full truckload of cans; 5,000 cases is equivalent to the amount of drink produced in a batch (it takes x amount of gallons depending on your drink's size [8, 10, 12, 16 ounces] and this usually equals enough to fill 5,000 cases).

There is the occasional bottler who will produce less than 5,000 cases, but then economies of scale start to take effect on your budget. In most instances, in order to keep costs at a constant you should go with 5,000 cans for your production runs. By doing this you start off right from the start with reasonable production costs, and it makes sense for all involved—for you, for the container manufacturer, and for the bottler.

Going back to the costing example, you now have your 8,000 cases of cans you have to pay for, plus you have to pay to fill 5,000 cases, plus the ingredients and raw materials that go into that. Using the example of the 16 ounce drink, an average size for an energy drink or functional beverage, you might pay $8 or $9 per case; depending on the vitamin pack and flavorings the figure could be from $7 to $9. To get the cost of your first production run you need to multiply that figure times 5,000, and then add in the cost of your additional 3,000 cases of unfilled cans.

This will give you roughly the amount of money the first investment in your energy drink/NAB production will require. Remember, this only covers production, though, and you also have to account for

- Research and development
- Sampling
- Labels
- POS materials
- Sales sheets
- Websites

All told the average cost of producing and launching your new age beverage will be between $60,000 and $85,000 (partially dependent on the size of the run, but also on ingredients and additives).

So finally, we arrive at a general figure to give you some idea of how much money it will take to launch your NAB--$60,000 to $85,000. Yes, we took the long road getting there, but it is important that you understand the big picture, made up of all the small and unforeseen costs, in order to really prepare you for a successful product launch and sustainable future in new age drink sales.

What to Do With All This Information?

Now you have figures and the ability to collect more accurate costing figures for your own beverage; what do you do with that information?

Once you have a costing figure and an idea of how large an investment it will take to launch your beverage, you have to go back and factor that into your planning. As the brand developer, you have important decisions to make.

These decisions go back to the consumer and to what they are willing to pay for a drink like yours. It could be anywhere between $1 and $3; you'll know this based on the market research you did initially in the beginning of your costing evaluation. Whatever that figure is you have to make the decisions that make sense for you, the consumer, and the retailer. What the consumer will pay dictates some of your options (including possible changes to the original product concept), and then you need to decide how to further distribute that money across each level (distributor, warehouse, retailer…). In the end, the practice of costing is all in the interest of planning.

Chapter 11

....

Beverage Development Overview

From here through the end of Part II, we'll focus on the nuts and bolts of product development. In this chapter we'll overview the major points, and then we'll take each in sequence and break them down to the last detail. By the end of the second part of this book, you'll have the whole of the picture of new age drink production. This part of the book will lay the groundwork for all of those components we discussed in the previous chapter on costing, and set you up for the last piece of the puzzle—marketing, selling, and distributing your drink—which will be broken down in the third and final part of the book.

Now, we'll take a brief look at these various components of product development, each of which will be covered in the chapters to come. Taken as a whole these components outline the steps of product development from concept to sales, effectively paving the way to success with your new age beverage.

Your Concept

Your Drink concept is your idea, your vision, your goal; this is your big-picture view of not only your product but of your whole company. We'll talk about how to focus in on your concept, how to develop it, and how to use it to develop your drink. To do this, we'll go through each and every step to drink production.

Target Market

Pinpointing your target market is the essential first step into product development and marketing. Target market is a concept many are familiar with as a marketing element, but your target market needs to be decided and researched early on so that you can develop a product that can sell. You cannot work on your product concept or packaging until you have decided who you will be selling it to.

We said it once, twice, and many times. This is your most important point in beverage development. It's not your formula or your package, it's your target market. Spend the most time here, understanding who are your consumers, your distributors and your retailers. Develop your Unique Selling and Unique Value Propositions to see how each segment of your supply chain will benefit.

Package & Look and Feel

Packaging may be a very practical and physical component, but it is what dictates the look and feel and perception of your product. This chapter will discuss how packaging and the look and feel of your drink plays into its success. We'll talk about the different considerations that go into making these important decisions and about a variety of options that you have to create your drink's look.

Taste

Great drinks are about great taste, right? Great drinks are, but *top selling* drinks are not always. Taste is a very important component in developing a drink that will be long-lived; for the new beverages coming on the market, taste will take on a new importance as the increased competition and familiarity with new and innovative beverages will dictate that now not only should drinks *function*, but they should function and *taste good*. We'll walk you through the process of developing the taste of your new product, and help you make sure that is a taste that is in line with the rest of your product's perception.

Production

When it's all said and done and all the planning is complete, you need to move your drink into production. You'll learn the process of production and all about outsourcing the various elements of new age drink production.

Most likely production of your beverage will be mechanic. You'll contact a co-packer and they will do all the work for you. In some special projects you'll own you production. Maybe you have a brewery or a distillery. If you own your production facility make sure you include it in your marketing propositions and use it to sell your product. You'll be one of the few brands that owns production, so it should be part of your selling proposition.

From Concept to Production

Once you've learned about all of these components, you'll be armed with everything you need up until and through the point of production. No doubt by the end of Part II you'll be eager to go, but we caution you to hold off just a bit longer. You'll be ready now to make a drink, but you won't be ready to sell it until you let us break down the rest of the picture in Part III. But for now, let's get into the nuts and bolts of drink production, so that you have a firm handle on this very important part of the business as each component applies at this stage.

Chapter 12

....

Beverage Concept

The quick explanation of what your beverage concept is, is that your concept is the big picture view of

1. Your drink and
2. Your company

This chapter is devoted to developing that overall perception that will guide not only this first drink, but also any others that come into your line as your company gains a following and becomes more successful.

More than Drink Flavors

Your concept is more than just the type of drink you want to sell; it's everything about your drink and your company that explains who you are and what you sell, and even how you sell it. Once you've developed your product concept, you'll have answered some very important questions, like:

- What do you sell?
- How do you sell it?
- How much do you sell it for?
- What is your goal?

The trick to developing your product and company concept is to start at the end—again, reverse engineering. You need to walk yourself backwards through time from that vision of a drink back to the first step in producing it. When you get back here, you'll have a full view of what your product and your company is to be.

The Elevator Pitch

A good way to start developing your concept is to develop your elevator pitch. For those of you not familiar with an elevator pitch, it is a quick summary about your business. The point is to be able to explain in about 30 seconds to one minute (about the span of an elevator ride) what you do. In the real world your elevator pitch does two things:

- It gives you a fast and reliable marketing tool that you can use at the drop of a hat
- It shows people that you are a focused, articulate, and informed businessperson who really means to succeed!

We ask you to start by developing your elevator pitch to give yourself the same focus and direction. What we want to do here is come up with one quick response that will explain your whole project quickly and effectively. Start by answering a few questions:

- Who are you?
- What do you do?
- What is your product?
- What does it do for your customer?
- How do you sell it?

Initially, your elevator pitch might sound something like:

"I'm the owner of XYZ Energy Drinks; I produce a healthy organic energy drink for women which I sell directly through drop shipping. We use public relations and magazine advertising to promote the health benefits of our drinks and their ingredients, and supply healthy, energy-boosting drinks specifically designed to meet the needs of women. We currently ship to 1,000 customers per month in the USA and Canada."

When you can answer all of these things in 100 words or less, you can succinctly portray your complete concept to yourself and to interested buyers and investors. For our purposes here, your elevator pitch serves as the first vision to who you want to be and what you want to do with your drink company. It stands as the first goal you've set for yourself and your product.

The Vision of Success

The easiest way we can develop your drink concept is to start with a vision of what your drink will be. Let's start with a vision—your vision (you're the visionary with the motivation and creativity to develop this drink)—your vision of your drink in the hands of your end consumer. Imagine someone actually drinking your beverage.

- Who is he (she)?
- What is he drinking?
- How old is she?
- What's the target market?
    - o Are they kids?
    - o Is this a children's drink?
    - o Is it for young adults? Seniors? Men? Athletes?

Next take a step back and think about where your consumer got this drink.
- Where did he buy it?
- Did he buy it? Did his mother or father buy it for him?
- Was it bought at a convenience store or gas station?

- Is it a specialty product sold only at auto parts stores or bars, at a gym, a health store, natural foods market, a supplement and vitamin store?
- Did a parent buy it in bulk for the family at Costco or the supermarket?
- Was it drop-shipped from a website?
- Was it sold through multi-level marketing?

Going through this list like this you can see all the very many, many possibilities for marketing and selling your beverage. Having all of this decided ahead of time will help you to start narrowing down the possibilities for distribution, sales, packaging, and marketing. And now that we have a clear vision of your product, we can use it to back-track through product development until we have the information we need to proceed with planning and drink production.

Walking Back Through Product Development to Product Concept

Now that we've summarized the big picture, we need to break it down into details and plans that will serve as the frameworks for a detailed business plan—your roadmap to product launch. What follows in the next several chapters is a walk back through the engineering process, starting as we did here with the end-product, and then analyzing even further to give us more specifics about your drink's concept. We'll spend a chapter walking backwards through each of the following, until we have the full picture of your product concept. These will include:

- Package look & feel
- Ingredients & taste
- Production
- Warehousing & logistics

Each of these components contribute to the development of your concept and by breaking them down each in their own chapter we guide you through the stages of developing your drink to where you can formalize it in the form of a business plan, and then on to actual production. Let's get started by taking a step back from that vision of your drink in your customer's hand to take a look at your product packaging, look and feel.

Chapter 13

....

Target Market

TARGET MARKET

Diagram 2.3 – Target Market

To define your target market, we need to expand on the idea we developed in the last chapter; we need to go back to that list of questions we asked when you were envisioning that consumer drinking your beverage. We need to know just who that person is, and then we need to find out what they are drinking and how we can reach them. We need to know everything we can about your target market so that we know just how to fulfill their beverage and refreshment needs.

I'm the Consumer

It's essential to know who your consumer is so that you know where and how to reach him. How else can you serve the needs of an entire segment or generation unless you clearly define those needs first?

We must be clear here that your target market is *not you*. It is *your consumer*. A great many drink developers would never drink their own product if it wasn't theirs; why? Because it wasn't made for them. We have doctors and attorneys and investors here who would never buy their product simply because it is not made for them. It is made for their target market. What this means is that you cannot just design a drink you like, you have to design a drink your *target market* likes. You do this by thinking like a marketer and putting yourself in your consumer's shoes.

My co-author Carlos López runs his clients through an exercise he calls, "I'm the Consumer." He uses the exercise to help our callers get a firm grasp on who their target market is.

What Carlos asksclients to do is just what we discussed before—sit down and envision the consumer drinking the product. Imagine that you are that consumer. Now, put yourself in her place and ask yourself some questions. Say to yourself, "okay, this product is intended for me, this person, so..."

- What do I need from this product?
- What functions do I want the drink to have?
- Why am I going to pick this product off the shelf?
- Why will I buy this product?

Reflect beyond the taste and function of the product (although you must give these their due, too) and figure out what it is this manufacturer is doing that makes you buy this product. Is it something about the packaging? The price? Is the flavor right for you?

You'll find out in the next chapter that the answers to these questions dictate a lot about packaging, but it goes far beyond that, too. This is a great exercise you can do with a simple piece of paper. It's a must for any new beverage project.

Besides using Carlo's exercise I like to imagine my target consumer. I imagine their name, nationality, age, income, where they go to school, what they want from life, their goals, and their motivations. Yes, it's like developing a character in a novel. What I try to accomplish is to think like my consumer. Pay special attention to financial factors of your consumer. How much do they make, where they shop and how much can they spend is crucial to figuring out your retail price. Don't price your product according to your costs, or what you think is "a good price". You have to get this form your perfect or alpha consumer.

If your target market is a 7 year old child, think not only about the child but the mother, the father, brothers and sister. Who buys beverages in the household? Is it the mother? Does she buy organic or saves money bu buying bulk? Develop a "protagonist" in your own beverage story. Get in your customer's head and see what motivates them.

Where Does Your Consumer Shop?

One of the things that the "I'm the Consumer" exercise will tell you is where and how to sell your product. You need to be thinking about not just *what* your consumer wants, but *who* is buying it (the consumer themselves, a parent, the woman of the house) and where they shop for beverages. You need to know this in order to know how to pack the product (singly, in six-packs, cases) and what distribution and retail channels will get your drink to your consumer. Once you know the answers to those questions a lot of your work is done and you can focus on meeting the needs of your consumers and establishing distribution channels to reach them.

Where your consumer shops can give you much more insight into your business than just the retail price or consumer background. It will dictate your distribution channel. Once you know where your consumer shops you know how to get the product to that retail store. Now you only have to contact the distributors that service that particular account. That simple. You get all of this from basic consumer research. Not only that, you'll know the profit margins for both your retailer and your distributor. A convenience store, supermarket, natural store, gym, or superstore or wholesale bulk store all make a different margin.

Researching Your Target Market

Researching your target market involves both grassroots efforts and market research. You should look to sources such as industry reports to study the trends in the various drink markets and study the trends for the demographics in your target market. You should look at the potential within your market, the size of it, and the amount of competition. Know, though, that this doesn't mean a smaller market is not a good place to be. In fact, niche drinks in niche markets that serve a very direct purpose do very well. Every one of you should be focusing on a niche, as that is how you will create appeal.

Don't forget what we talked about earlier in terms of good old-fashioned face-to-face research, too. Get out on the street and talk to these consumers, find out what they are drinking and why, and what else they might be looking for. You can also, again, talk to distributors and retailers and find out who is buying what, and then look into the big sellers for your market.

Later on in the development of your product you will take your target market research a step further. You will look to focus groups to gather information and try your product out on. They'll test your product and answer your questions.

All of this—target market research, demographics, focus groups—is in an effort to get your drink as on-target as possible the first time around. There is a good chance that you'll make some changes along the way to really meet the needs of your target market, but with good research to begin with you'll be able to avoid a lot of remanufacturing and repacking. That is essential to the success and profitability of your drink, as every added step and remanufacturer is another thing that will drive up the cost of your drink development and production before you get to the point of selling.

Ready to Go On

You now know the most important piece of information you need to have in order to move forward with drink development and production—you know who you are developing your drink for. Now that you know that, you can keep coming back to your defined target market to make every decision from the size of the drink to the cap on the top—everything that will make your NAB function for your consumer in the way that it should. The way that sells!

Chapter 14

....

Package & Look and Feel

You now know who will buy your product, your target market. Now it's time to visualize your product. How will it look and feel in your hand, on the shelf and in the refrigerator. What size will it be, will you use a bottle or can, will the bottle be plastic or glass.

Packaging for Your Consumer

With the vision of who the product is for firmly in mind, we need to choose packaging that will appeal to them and also function as per the function of the beverage. For example, if your beverage is designed to be a drink for runners, it should be packaged in plastic as opposed to glass or aluminum; it should have an easy-access, no-spill sport cap and not a screw-off top so that it can literally be drunk "on the run."

Let's get a bit technical and explore the different components of your package. Some of them will be too specific for an executive and more suited for a designer or project manager, but it's a good idea for you to see the different options and get a better idea of how packaging works. You have a few basic options for each component of the actual container and cap.

Tops

Tops will vary in cost and the type of top you choose will depend once again on the intended use and your target market. There are four basic options:

- Flat top; this is your basic, standard flat screw top you see on plastic water bottles, soda bottles, and the like; there is a range of sizes and flat tops are available in just about any color you can dream up.
- Sport top; sport top versions of drink tops come in all manner of shapes, sizes, and colors. More elaborate tops can control back-flow and accidental spills, and others are even ergonomically shaped to match the shape of your mouth. As you can see the variety is enormous and the costs will definitely reflect the creativity.
- Metal top; these tops, used in conjunction with glass bottles, are either mechanically screwed on or pneumatically forced on. An example of a forced bottle cap is what is found on most glass beer bottles; they can either be removed with a bottle opener or twisted off. Other examples of metal caps and tops are those found on products like Snapple; metal tops like these are always lined with some sort of plastic or other material that helps keep the built-up pressure inside.
- Can tops; tops on cans, as you can imagine, don't vary as much as tops on bottles. The choices really have not evolved as much as one might expect, even from the beginning of beverage can production, leastwise not in terms of the actual look; technically can tops have advanced. Today the choices would include just a few items like a specially colored tab, or a tab with a cutout that adds to the branding of the beverage. Just recently we've seen tops that make a sound when opened but these have not yet made an impact in the overall market. Other than these few, the choices with can tabs are limited.

Containers

We could spend pages and pages going over the variety of containers available for beverages today. There are entire publications devoted to nothing but drink containers. There is a lot of attention placed on containers because drink containers make a very significant impact on the product's overall success. The container is emphasized more than anything else, and it is a huge factor in your cost.

For containers you have three basics options:

- Glass
- Plastic
- Aluminum

Of these materials the choices are basically bottle or can (noting that even aluminum is being used for some bottles). However, there are a couple of other options that have been used primarily for kids' drinks, but that are now seeing use by a variety of products, such as:

- Pouches—made from aluminum, lined with plastics & other materials, similar to Capri Sun packaging. Popular for kids' beverages and convenient for lunchboxes, these often come 10 or 12 to a box; warehouse stores (Costco, Sam's Club) will often sell four to six boxes at a time.

  Pouches are enjoying a resurgence in popularity, and are getting very big in the Orient.

- Tetra Pack—made from a cardboard application (similar to traditional juice boxes), tetra packs extend shelf-life by preserving the package contents and protecting it from the outside environment. Tetra bricks are now being used for grocery items like tomato sauce, too.

Whatever material you choose for your beverage, realize that the material it is made from will be very influential to sales. For example, glass is very heavy and expensive, and breaks easily, which makes it a poor choice for functional sports beverages and usually children's beverages. On the other hand, glass can put a product in a different category, often as a more adult or sophisticated drink that sells for more. As an example, a lot of new waters typically demand a higher price for glass-packed products, and they also ship less; therefore, they cost more to produce, but brands have been able to use glass as a way to differentiate and charge more.

Bottles (including plastic and aluminum) are often chosen by companies as a way to be unique; while it is easy to come up with a unique label it is much harder to come up with your own unique bottle. There are different variations of this; many big drink companies will pay artisan crafters to produce their own molds, but those are for liquors that are selling for $30-$60 off the shelf. Unless you are one of them you'll have to go with a bottle off the shelf, since engineering costs on a custom bottle can be between $30,000 and $50,000, plus engineering costs.

In addition, even for off-the shelf containers, you have customizable options within each category (can, bottle...). Every custom addition adds to the cost, though, and these options are mostly limited to very well-funded beverage companies.

To start you will definitely want to forgo that expense and go with a product off the shelf. There are more than enough choices to be unique just by working with the standard options and changing them up through labeling and design.

We've talked a lot about bottles; now let's take a minute to look at cans.

The can category has been expanding quite a bit lately. It used to be that there was only your basic 12 ounce can and nothing more. Today there is a range of sizes and even a few new shapes and variations. One of the most unique options in cans is custom shapes, such as the keg-shaped cans Heineken has produced, and aluminum bottles. Next to this, the only difference is really in the size of the can, and the shape stays basically the same. There is a can size to fit every drink concept—4 ounce, 6 oz., 8.4, 11.5, 16, 24, 32 oz...

Each shape and size has its own advantages and you will choose based upon the function and concept of your drink. For example, aluminum bottles can't be resealed and used like a glass bottle, but will be accepted in certain venues (such as sports stadiums) where glass is not allowed for safety. Small cans of 4 ounces or 6 ounces are sleek and sophisticated, and can give the perception of 'bang for the buck.' You can use the different can options to your advantage as you develop your brand and concept.

In the U.S. there are two major manufacturers of cans; those are Ball and Rexam. There are a limited number of plants that can produce the custom-shaped cans, but here again that is probably irrelevant at this point as you will be better off starting with a more affordable standard can.

Labels

The label is just as important as the container and is a strong differentiating point. Labels communicate to the seller; they spell out quality, price, function, and more.

There are many different labeling options. There are:

- Plastic standard wrap—plastic labels are most notably used for their resistance to the environment they will be subject to, such as refrigerators, coolers, etc.

- Paper –glue-front and glued around—very limited use, although inexpensive; the more colors you add on paper the more expensive the label

- Metal/silk-screening—prints directly on the can and is durable against elements; up until now, this has been the only real option for cans. It's fairly affordable, but silk screening has its limitations; silk screening is limited in graphics, attractiveness, colors, shades, and tones, and requires a large printing run (on average, you'll be required to print 8,000 cases per run).

- Shrink wrap—shrink wraps are plastic labels that encase the entire container. They can be used on bottles or cans. Shrink wraps can be printed to include almost any graphics, colors, or shades. The printed wrap encases a blank can or bottle, then is heated and shrinks to fit. Designing a shrink wrap is more expensive at first, but once set up shrink wraps are inexpensive in the long run.

This completes the list of options in terms of packaging. You need to choose the right options to meet the functional needs of your drink, and to present the look and feel that will appeal to your target market. Achieving the right packaging with the right presentation is essential to success, so that at a glance your consumer can see which product has paid attention to their wants and needs, and is likely to be the drink they are looking for.

Chapter 15

....

Ingredients & Taste

With the look and feel and packaging of your product under control, you can focus on what's inside. Now is the time to start picking ingredients and flavors and developing the taste of your drink. Like packaging, your ingredients and taste will go back to the envisioned concept and function of your drink.

Choosing Your Flavor Profile

You may already have an idea for your drink's taste. Perhaps you have even profiled the ingredients and created your drink's recipe. Some of you may even have your drink's profile, taste, and ingredients all in place, and have just come here looking to develop the rest of the profile.

If your drink's profile is in the 'idea' stage, you're likely wondering where to go to create the profile of your drink. Even those of you who have developed your drink's profile are urged to read this chapter, as there is essential information in it that will impact the concept of your product, and help you in developing your brand.

To develop your flavor profile—the tastes and raw ingredients that will go into your drink—you will be working with a flavor house. The flavor house will have access to all of the various flavors and raw materials that will go into your drink, and can work with you to determine the right balance of each to create a great tasting new age beverage. What you will need is a clear vision of your drink to guide them and to help in choosing the right flavors and ingredients.

The first step in working to achieve that taste is to select the right flavor house for your needs. Keep in mind that not all flavor houses deal in the same types of ingredients and products; so, for example, if you will be developing an all natural or organic drink, you need to find a flavor house that can provide products that can rightfully be labeled as such. Likewise, if you are looking for artificial sweeteners such as those used in diet drinks, or artificial flavors similar to those used in sodas, you will want to find the flavor house that works primarily with those types of ingredients. Finally, if you are looking to create a drink with new and exotic flavors, that is what you want to search out. By now surely you sense a theme—you need a flavor house capable of servicing your needs; ask questions first, not later, and save yourself a lot of aggravation by considering the options ahead of time.

Choosing the Flavors

There is only one way to know which flavor house can suit your needs. That way is to first determine what your flavor and ingredients needs are. At the risk of sounding like a broken record, this goes back to the function of your drink.

What you need to do first is brainstorm your drink, its concept and function as far as you know to this point. Then you have to match that to the flavors that you think will serve that need. If you are unsure, get clear on your concept, do some research and find out what similar drinks are offering, and ask questions of sellers and the flavor house.

As you go through the process of choosing flavors and ingredients for your drink, think about what your target consumer wants in his or her drink. Let's take a look at a few examples:

- The health conscious consumer will be looking for a drink that gives them added health benefits; give him vitamins and minerals—something to help meet his daily requirements. Bear in mind this person does not want a lot of unhealthy ingredients added, so sugars may not be the way to go. But what about artificial sweeteners? Maybe and maybe not, depending on how far you intend to take the health angle.

- The all-natural consumer will most certainly not want fake sweeteners in her drink. This buyer will look more for the ingredients Mother Nature intended, and care less about what they'll do to their waistline. Flavors here will have to be convincing, not made up of ingredients that don't sound 'real'. There are all natural drinks that can actually be higher in calories but still meet consumer needs as long as they feel good about drinking them.

- The runner or athlete may think little of either of these factors, and just want to get what they need to perform. That could be an electrolyte pack or hydrating agent.

- The organic buyer will be similar to the natural buyer, but want something that can legally carry a certification so that they can feel more secure about drinking your product. Keep in mind the organic flavor house has to be able to meet those standards, regardless of the flavor.

- The consumer looking for something hot and sexy will be looking for exotic flavors. These will be more than your run-of-the-mill fruit flavors, something more uncommon and less mainstream.

- The energy drink consumer of today is just looking for a jolt; high caffeine has often been the order of the day. But as the category ages, the healthy energy drinker is emerging, and will be looking for natural boosts that are a little better for them.

Understand that these are just examples to jog your thinking. There are many variations and combinations of each, creating niche markets for functional drinks or other new beverage categories. This is precisely what you want to do to make your drink as appealing to your crowd as possible, so that it very specifically meets their demands.

As you can see there are many angles to take towards flavoring and ingredient profiling. At the end of the day it all comes down to finding the right flavor house to be your partner and supplier. Work with them, but always keep your mission in mind, and develop the right balance between flavor and ingredients so that neither will offend your customer. Remember that while flavor may prevail as the obvious draw, ingredients are equally important to the choosy consumer who is looking to get the definite advantage of the function of your drink.

Chapter 16

....

Production

We have a drink profile; we know our flavors; we know what we will be putting our beverage in—we know the look, feel, taste, and composition of our new age beverage. The next step is to get it produced—bottled! For that, we look to the bottling facility.

What Can Your Bottler Do For You?

As we said earlier in the book, bottling is a job you will definitely want to outsource. It is an absolute misconception that you have to have your own bottling facility in order to produce your own new age beverage. It would be a gross misappropriation of funding to put money into building a bottling plant when there are literally thousands of them out there whose sole business is to co-pack beverage products for others.

Like finding the right flavor house, though, finding the right bottler takes some foot-work. All bottlers do not handle the same type of bottling or use the same types of processes. Not all can handle the same types of containers, or produce specialty products to certification standards. Different facilities will have different capabilities; some can produce hot-fill products, others only cold-fill, some can produce natural and organic products, others cannot; some can only bottle into cans, others plastic or glass. So you see, not all bottlers can process your hot-fill natural tea in an aluminum can; you'll have to find out first which bottlers can handle which containers and processes.

A Bottler for Every NAB

As reported by *Beverage World* magazine, the rise in new age beverages and "craft beers" has contributed to increased availability of co-pack processers and various processing options. *Beverage World* credited the new age beverage market with changing the co-packing 'game'.[9] They report that small start-up companies in particular have more reason to seek a co-packing arrangement, and that the co-pack industry has opened opportunities in new age beverage production that otherwise would be difficult to achieve. They have compiled a list of processers across the U.S. and Canada, complete with contact information, and included the processing capacities of each, broken into the following categories:

- Cold fill
- Retort
- Purepak
- Aseptic
- Hot fill
- Tunnel

This is a convenient reference for those looking for specific processing needs; you can access it through *Beverage World*, or you can contact us if you need help finding bottling solutions.

Steps in the Production Process

To give you an idea of how this process will work, we'll run you through a very quick and abbreviated process from production through bottling. For this exercise, let's assume that you've gotten through concept development and research, and you are ready to put your order into the various partnering businesses you have chosen to work with (let's also assume you've asked all the right questions, and you know that these are the professionals that can meet your needs).

- First, you order your containers and labels.

- Next, you order all of your flavoring and raw materials (ingredients) (note, some bottlers will do this after you've scheduled your production run).

- You call your bottler and schedule a production run; plan ahead, it will probably be 30 to 40 days or more before your run can be produced.

- Inform suppliers of production dates, and have supplies (containers, labels, ingredients and flavoring) shipped to your bottler.

- Your drink will be produced on the scheduled date.

Be aware that once the run is produced you will need to have arrangements in place for storage until distribution—you need to have arranged warehousing.

This is a short and sweet chapter because the bottling of your product is primarily handled by the bottler you choose. You, of course, have to make sure that all preparations for prior to and after bottling are completed; and more importantly you need to do your due diligence and choose the right bottler for your product. These are the major points we need you to take away from this chapter. Though they are few, they are fundamental to producing your drink. And now that we're done we need to move on to the next chapter to discuss the warehousing and logistics that need be in place once your bottler is finished with your co-packed product.

Chapter 17

....

Warehousing & Logistics

Warehousing can be something of a tricky subject and in fact many drink developers do not realize that there is a need for warehousing at all, assuming that to be the job of the distributor. What is not commonly understood is that product does not go directly from the production plant to the distributor, and so you will need to make arrangements for storage in the interim. For this, you have a couple of options, but primarily we will focus on the best solution for new drink developers.

Basic Options for Beverage Warehousing

There are three basic options for warehousing your beverages. You can

- Build/maintain your own warehousing facility (not likely cost-effective)

- Rely on small, private storage units (of limited usefulness, but can serve a purpose, as we'll discuss)

- Use a third-party warehouse (the best solution for small beverage companies)

We'll focus mostly on the third-party warehouse, or 3PL, but also discuss the role a small storage unit can play in your warehousing needs, and why it is not advantageous to maintain your own warehouse facility.

The Third Party Warehousing Arrangement

The easiest and most inexpensive warehousing arrangement is to use a third party warehouse, also referred to as logistics warehousing, third party logistics, or 3PL. A third party warehousing arrangement is one where you take your product (have it transported) to a controlled warehousing facility and pay rent per pallet, per month.

The average cost of 3PL warehouse storage runs between $8 and $12 per pallet, per month. You can get better deals depending on where you are in the country, on how many pallets you are storing, and depending on your relationship with the warehouse, but this is a good ball-park figure for planning purposes.

It's interesting to note here, too, that you don't have to be small, or be a small company to use a third party warehouse. A lot of large beverage companies use 3PL's because they have their own offices, but not offices with warehouse facilities. This may not apply to you if you are a distributor, as you will for sure have your own warehouse facilities in which to store your product at no additional cost; that's a great advantage to you, but most of the visionaries here reading this book do not have that kind of access, and that's completely alright.

3PL & Warehousing Costing Considerations

To accurately plan costing for a 3PL facility, you need to have an understanding of what is and is not included in your rental fee. The base fee for 3PL storage covers only the receiving of your product and its removal out of the facility. That fee covers nothing else. Therefore, if you have to have a partial order shipped out, have to move or break pallets or cases, have products drop-shipped, or do anything else with your product you will pay an extra fee. So, for example, if you have to start sending samples and need to start taking cases out, that could be extra; if you want the warehouse to send one or two cases of samples for you that will cost extra. Anything that makes more work for the warehouse on top of receiving and removal will add to your basic rental cost.

You cannot assume that you'll ship a full truckload of product every time you sell to a distributor. You may have 22 pallets in the warehouse but may only sell one or a few at a time. So if there are 22 pallets in the warehouse you have to pay a fee to have them moved in (received), and then you have to pay again for each shipment, each time product leaves the facility. It's an incremental cost, and one that must be accounted for.

This may make it sound like a 3PL could nickel and dime you to death, but you need to put this into perspective. The intention here is not to scare you off of a 3PL—not at all; it is simply to make you aware of the factors that go into warehouse costing so that you plan and budget accordingly.

Your only realistic alternative to a 3PL is maintaining your own warehouse facility (owning or renting). However, it's not smart to pay rent on your own warehouse if you really don't need it; it's much more cost effective to go with a 3PL facility than to try to consume the expense of your own warehouse space. If you only have to store two or three containers or 5,000 cases of product and you are looking at renting, then for that it's much easier and reasonable to save money and use a third party warehouse. There's no need to pay rent at a rate of three, four, or up to ten thousand dollars just to call the warehouse your own.

Let us break this down to clarify why 3PL is the way to go.

Rental of a warehouse only covers the actual real estate cost. There are many other costs that go along on top of that, and those get very expensive, very quickly. In order to maintain your own warehouse you would have to assume the entire cost of everything that goes along with it—everything the 3PL provides. With the 3PL, the costs are dispersed among all clients; in your own facility, they are all yours. You would have to hire a warehouse manager—someone to control and open and close the warehouse; you would need a security system; you'd need to own or lease equipment to move product on and off trucks and around the warehouse; on top of these major expenses you have operational expenses including telephone, office management, electricity, climate and environmental control (heating, refrigeration), and others.

Clearly these costs make the added costs of 3PL services pale in comparison. To make a long story short, logistics warehousing is most always the right solution for a start-up NAB producer.

The Role of Private Storage Units

There is one other arrangement we should take a minute to mention. This is by no means a total warehousing solution, but it is one that can help defray the costs of 3PL warehouse fees if you will need access to product for the purposes of sampling and so on.

What many drink developers do—especially in the beginning when they need frequent access to small amounts of product—is to rent a small private storage unit and store a few pallets there. This gives quick and easy access to product for sampling and drop-shipping without incurring the expense of warehouse services each time. The bulk of the product is safely stored at the 3PL, and a mini storage unit is used in addition to it.

Concept Complete, Moving On

This completes the discussion on warehousing, as well as the discussion on concept. We have now looked at every factor that you need to consider to develop your business concept and give you that big-picture view of who you are, what you do, who you serve, and how you serve them. We do have a few more parts that relate to concept that we need to explore in depth, but as these are also essential to the sales, distribution, and marketing end of the business, we will take the conversation over to Part III of the book.

Before we move on to Part III, though, we would like to take the opportunity to interject and present you with another option that can help you start your business and minimize some of these costs through some special production programs we have developed at Liquid Brands Management, Inc. Join us in the next chapter and we'll discuss some ways that you can get into the business of developing a new age beverage and diminish the investment burden.

PART THREE

MARKETING, SELLING, AND DISTRIBUTING YOUR DRINKS

Chapter 18

....

Introduction to Marketing, Selling, & Distributing Your Drinks

We move on now to the third and final part of our book. This is the part of the book that focuses on the sales, distribution, and marketing of your beverage.

Is there a magic bullet for success in your beverage business? Yes, there is!

I know, you were expecting a "No, its hard work and you need to do 20 things to be successful". Actually, there is one thing that just about ensures your success in the beverage industry and in other consumer goods and even service industries. Do you know it? **It's developing an emotional connection with your consumer.**

Even without millions of dollars in advertising, large promotional teams, trade show budgets and major national beverage distributors, if you have an emotional connection with your consumer that person will look for your product and buy it. It doesn't matter if you sell it in a 7-Eleven, on the internet or out of your garage. People will find you and buy your product.

The use of the internet and mass media make it possible for you to reach out to your perfect consumer and make connections. Tell them about you, your product and your beverages. This is why you see Coke's old commercials come back every few years, because they're making that emotional connection based on the past. You don't have the luxury of appealing to past consumers with your beverage so you have to create new connections.

How can you create new emotional connections? My favorite way is to tie products to social causes and becoming a social entrepreneur. Every time you have a new consumer or a new sale, they are making a difference in the world. I tie my products to my charity for children in Mexico.

You can create your own charity or tie it to an existing charity. Its good business and just plain good. People will respond to a cause much better than just responding to a product. It's not easy to make an emotional connection with a product, a thing, but it's easy to make it with a person. If your consumers can change the life of a child by sending them to school just by buying your product it's a very easy way to incorporate them into your business model.

Stay in contact with your consumers. If you want to make that emotional connection make sure you use email, social media, mail, and other tools to keep in touch with your consumer. Don't just tell them you donated 5% to charity, send them a picture of the school, or children, or the people you're helping.

Many parts of marketing, sales and distribution are mechanical and formulaic, but establishing a relationship with your consumer, a consumer marketing activity, is not. It takes creativity, planning, good value propositions and timing.

The Most Value for Your Time and Money

This is the part of the business where most beverage producers and executives fall short. But because we rise to face the most difficult task head-on, this is the part where you get the most value and benefit—as our reader and as a drink developer, executive or entrepreneur. By showing you not just how to get a drink bottled, but how to, more importantly, get your target market buying that drink by the caseload.

All drinks that fail, fail in sales and distribution. This is important for you to know. Beverage development is easy, marketing, sales and distribution, not so much. Most new beverage entrepreneurs and executives have a hard time understanding where their drink failed—they created the best tasting drink the industry has seen; they created the most attractive packaging for their drink; they have the best look and design; they have the whole package, but they have no sales.

Most new beverage developers thought people were going to ask them about purchasing their drink because they read about it or saw it on the internet. Then they come to the harsh realization that their consumers need to be communicated with in a certain way: "This is my product, this is what it's all about, and this is where I want to sell it." Distributors need to know that and retailers need to know that; and they both need to know that there is an eager market out there ready to buy your drink. But still, developers forget that they need to get out there and market this drink to all of these factions in order to make it a success.

The average drink developer seriously underestimates the role that the retailer, distributor, and other essential personnel play in the success of any given drink. All the brands that we see as consumers we only pick up because we've been educated about them in some way—we heard about them, read about them, there were sales reps going door to door introducing and pushing them. And it's the people who are doing these things that are making brands what they are today.

Many people forget that it's what happens after a drink is off the production line that makes it profitable. Anyone can manufacture a product on any given day. Anyone can come up with a great tasting product. It takes a real marketer who is going to get a product where it needs to be on the shelves, and get it in the hands of the consumer. That's where a drink will either fail or succeed. That's where you will succeed because you have this information now, when it matters most.

If the entire process from development to consumer were a 10-step process, getting the drink produced and bottled is probably only the first step. There are 9 more to go before you have a product that is selling and making you money. That's the span that's covered in the rest of this book.

The Harsh Reality

The harsh reality of the business is that a large majority of the drinks that are produced are never successful. The reason for that is that they are never effectively marketed—there was never an effective marketing and business plan, and so there was no way to communicate and get the consumer to buy (if that consumer ever actually saw the product at all).

When we take into account the number of drink brands that have gone through the development phase, even just the number of drink brands that we have been involved in, and look to see how many have actually become successes, we begin to see how critical this part of the business is. Sadly, many of these are drinks that we worked closely with. Just in our experience alone we have had numerous drinks come through where we've walked the developers through from just an infant of an idea to a promising, full-fledged product ready for market, only to have the developers insist that that part of development was all we were needed for. Every time, we've tried to impress upon them the importance of the next step, but these developers would persist and tell us they had it covered—they had a singer, or a friend in the movie industry, or some advantage that was going to turn this product into the product of their dreams. In the end, only about 10% of the drinks succeed and become profitable; all for a lack of a definitive business plan and a course of marketing action.

Stepping Back to Business 101

We've worked hard to impress upon you the importance of a solid plan for your business, sales, distribution, and marketing. This is what the last part of this book is here to help you with. Let's stress again how important it is to have a great sales strategy and answer every question so that you know how to get from point A to point B.

To develop that plan we will take a walk backwards from the end consumer to your product—just as we did to develop the product and tell you how to make the right choices and accommodate for each financially along the way.

You'll learn what the channels for distribution and sales are and how to get into the right ones. We will also tell you what you don't know about selling your drink—what your responsibilities are and what your retailers and distributors need from you. We'll talk about the options and help you identify which can work for you. Essentially, we'll take you through a course of Business 101 with an emphasis specifically on the beverage business, and we'll show you what others are missing so that you come out of this fully prepared to not only produce a drink (which again, anyone can do), but make the sales that make you money!

Chapter 19

....

Beverage Marketing Plan

What is your marketing plan? It's the roadmap for getting consumers to buy your product. If you're shipping your product directly to consumers, your marketing plan will include direct marketing, drop shipping, catalogs and price specials. If you're using convenience stores your marketing plan will probably have consumer marketing, trade marketing to convenience stores and distributors, and logistics. Your marketing plan should specify who your consumer is, your distribution model and how you'll sell it across the entire supply chain (for example: consumer, retailer distributor).

Here is a starting point for the creation of your marketing plan:

- Outline your marketing plan
- Distribution
- Defining and reaching your target market
- Competition
- Price strategy
- Understanding and developing your positioning statement
- Packaging (as it relates to marketing)
- Sales materials, including POS material and sale sheets
- Sales and distribution structure

- Promotions and advertising

Beverage Marketing Plan

Your new beverage *absolutely needs a marketing plan*!

Many people think that a marketing plan is not necessary. They think they will just wing it, or that they will figure it out as they go along; sometimes they think that if they just plan to spend big money in marketing then it will take care of itself. That is a way to spend a lot of money and a lot of time, and achieve very few results.

What happens is that when these producers are faced with the actual expenditure—either of time or money—they don't know where to start. At this point even if you do manage to identify your consumer, perhaps a distributor even, it will be too late; because there just will not be the mechanism in place to connect all of these fundamentals.

What really happens is that if you don't have a marketing plan it will be very difficult to put product in the hands of distributors, retailers, and consumers. What isn't well understood is that your marketing plan is really a guide that you will use to land those distributors, retailers, and consumers. Your marketing plan is not just your plan for advertising; it's not just a TV commercial or promotion; it is everything that involves the positioning of your brand, the selling of your brand, and the promotion of your brand, including pricing, sales, distribution, and many things in between.

The bottom line is this: make sure you have a marketing plan.

Starting from Scratch: Building Your Marketing Plan

By the time you have completed your marketing plan you will know many things. You will know:

1. What your expenditures per month or per distributor will be
2. How you will support your distributors
3. How much you will spend on retailers
4. How you will support your retailers
5. How ultimately you will reach out to your consumers and sell your product off the shelves

All of this very critical information will be found in your marketing plan. To answer those questions, we start from scratch, at the very beginning.

The starting point of your marketing plan will be your executive summary. This is a one to two page document that explains the whole marketing plan. You might also note, too, that the structure of your marketing plan also applies to your overall business plan; both follow the same standard structure.

Your marketing plan will also include information about your product—for example, photos, price points for your product, size, the look, why it exists…everything you can think about your product.

In addition, your marketing plan will include some very important budgetary information; all the financials relating to your brand support will be a part of the marketing plan. This will include how much you spend per month and per year in public relations, advertising, marketing…every cost involved in supporting the brand. This might also include sales data broken down by channel, customer, state, city, country, retailer, and distributor. The more financial information that is included in your marketing report the better. This becomes a highly useful tool for all involved, including investors and employees if or when you have them. These financials will serve as a roadmap for all to follow.

All marketing plans need to include information on pricing as well. This does not just mean the pricing to the consumer, but also your pricing, and the price to the retailer and distributor, too. Every tier of your pricing plan must be laid out in your marketing plan.

One often overlooked inclusion in your marketing plan will be information about your competition. Many new drink producers think that because they are a unique product or a newly created niche they will not have competition. However, *every* product has competition, and every successful drink developer will not only know that, but know who that competition is, and then include that as part of an effective marketing plan so that he or she knows how to strategize and compete against them.

Finally, you will talk about yourself—your background and experience—and also about your distribution channels.

All of this sounds like a lot, because it is. This is a great deal of information that you will be including in your marketing plan. And by including it, not only will you show to others that you have prepared and thoroughly researched the marketing and profitability of your drink, but you will also show that to yourself. Once you have covered all of these bases, you will be able to look back and see that you have laid a detailed roadmap for the success of your drink and your business.

That being said, you are not expected to have all of these answers right now. For the time being, you are only expected to be aware that you need to know these things eventually. As we progress through this chapter and the last part of this book, we will talk about each of these points in more detail, and give you the information that you need to research and make decisions to develop your marketing strategy.

Marketing Misconceptions

One of the reasons that people fail to create effective marketing plans is that they do not understand what marketing is. Marketing is all of those things we just discussed. It is not just about advertising.

There is a huge misconception that marketing is just about the face on the product. We see projects all the time from people who think they have their marketing plan all laid out because they have a singer or an athlete to back it; or they think that their marketing is complete because they've come up with a really great name or look, or because they are marketing to a specific audience like motocross or athletes.

There is no doubt that sponsoring a high-profile figure, or marketing to a targeted audience can be beneficial. To be sure we have spent a lot of time driving home the importance of knowing your target market, and that is one way to connect with them. But just putting that face out there is not enough. You have to step beyond that and really get to know your target market.

Having a spokesperson or an identity for your drink is a good first step, but it's only a first step. The next step is to look beyond that persona to learn about the actual identity of that target market.

Having a sponsor in mind does help give you a clearer idea of who your target market is going to be (which is not to say that you cannot accomplish that without a sponsor, either). For example, if you are appealing to the motocross rider then obviously you have an extreme product; it needs certain colors and graphics that will appeal to that type of person.

A sponsor or angle clearly points out who you are trying to approach with your products, and that identifies the end consumer. It gives you a starting point because it gives you answers to the important questions, like

- Who is your end consumer?
- Where does he or she buy their drink?
- What do they like to do?
- When?
- How frequently?

Having these answers starts defining the expenses that you will be incurring in order to get to that target market. To develop a true plan for marketing, though, you need to go beyond that starting point to the answers to these questions. Those are the answers that give you the details that can be translated into hard numbers, costs, expenses, and profits.

Exercises in Market Identification

Here is a fairly simple exercise that you can do to learn more about your target market and get those answers that you need.

Start by making a mental note and saying, "Okay, I have this beverage and it will be sold in a store." (Understanding that for some beverages the answer may not be a store, it could be a bar or restaurant, MLM or direct response, etc,).

Now you ask yourself some questions about that store or that place that will sell your beverage in case you're going with traditional distribution.

- What type of store is it? Is it a convenience store? Chain? Independent? A restaurant and not a store at all? Supermarket? Natural foods store? Or maybe a mass retail store? A pharmacy? Bar? Night club?

Then you start thinking about the type of customer you have and where they shop, start comparing that to where your product will be placed. Answer those questions first:

- What type of consumer do I have?
- Where do they shop?

And then go further

- How much money do they have?
- How much money do they make? (Or do they? Do parents give them their spending money? Or buy their products for them?)
- Are they men? Women? Teens? Aged 16-35?
- What kind of car do they drive?

Your list can, and should, go on and on until you have the most detailed vision of your clientele and how and when they buy beverages. Everything you do in marketing will be to attract those people, but also to attract the places that sell to them—the retailers and distributors that supply their drinks to them.

This is where we begin to identify the distribution channels that will be specific to your drink. Once you know the buyer and the target market you have to move backwards all the way back to your point of manufacture. Let's look at an example.

Let's suppose that you are selling tea—green tea or an iced tea. That is a product that you could sell at a convenience store refrigerator. So you have to ask yourself:

"How do I get a product into a convenience store refrigerator?"

There are a few possibilities; maybe you go to 7-Eleven at the corporate level, Circle K, or maybe other convenience stores nationally or by state and you sell them on your product. But then you need to answer this question:

"How will the product get to the store?"

Well, for that you need a distributor. So already you have determined that you have to sell the product to the convenience store itself, but also to a beverage distributor, wholesaler, or other type of distributor. But how do you know who to sell to? You have to go and find out who sells the product to the stores that you are selling to.

From here the next step backwards would be back to your manufacturing to source the product (this we have already done in the first two parts of the book); and so when you connect those two points what you have is a complete cycle all the way from your target market back to your manufacturing. As you can see now, your target market concept doesn't stop with your consumer, it stops at your manufacturer—with the types of vitamins, natural flavors, or other elements that you've chosen to serve that target market.

Putting Numbers to Your Target Market Profile

With the information we just garnered we can begin to put numbers to your marketing costs. We now know what that channel is at the end of your profile; whether that channel is a night club, a hotel, convenience store, retail store…whatever that sales outlet is will determine what your numbers are. Let's expand on that a bit to give you some idea of what you are looking at.

Basically we are still (almost always) talking target market. Since you know your target market you know that that customer is going to be at a supermarket or convenience store, for example, and so you know that you are going to have to travel; so you need a corporate account. Now you start setting up your budget profile and you say, "I need to make 12 visits per year at an average cost of $2,500 per visit, and I need to send two to three representatives per visit to supermarkets." You also figure you need 12 visits per year to convenience chains, and so you need to add to those costs: another $2,500 per representative, per trip. You can see how these costs begin to grow (and hence why the financials become so important). This is how your target market helps define how much money you are spending for every channel.

Sponsorships may be another marketing expense you have to determine. So for example, if you choose to sponsor a motocross rider to reach out to that target group, you will need a base figure to tell you what your costs for sponsoring will be for a year. But you need to keep in mind that in most cases when you sponsor you will be committed for two to three years in order to get the valuable space that will convert to sales. So not only do you have to determine the annual cost, but you have to prepare to carry that over a number of years.

Club events add another possibility and another level of costs. If your target market likes to go to clubs you'll need to include club events. For every city that you choose you will probably host one event every weekend, every month, at four locations. So that brings you to about 16 events per month, multiplied by the number of cities you've chosen. When you start putting numbers to those events you start realizing that events will cost you X amount of dollars, and that you need a staff of two or three people at each of your 16 events.

As you begin to harvest these numbers, you want to begin to track them in a way that helps build them into your plan. Start out very informally and make a list:

- This is my target market
- This is where they shop
- This is what I need to do to reach that market
- This is the frequency that needs to be done on an ongoing basis

This will result in real, hard numbers that you can begin to plug into your planning spreadsheets. As we go on, we'll add to those numbers once we start determining costs for things like Point of Sale materials and trade show exhibitions and so on.

Having the numbers is important for budgeting, but it also serves a planning purpose. Once you know what you are looking at you might decide that you have the funding to start with five markets at the same time or that you can only afford to start in your own backyard. Or, you might decide that whereas before you thought five investors would be enough, you really need 20. These are the numbers that will put the proof into your marketing plan, so that in the end you have an excellent plan that is capable of supporting your beverage.

Competition as a Marketing Factor

People hold many myths about competition. Some do not see it as a marketing factor; they categorize it elsewhere. Others do not think that they have competition because they have very specifically designed their product to serve a niche market. Neither of these is ever the case—there is always competition, and it is always a factor that impacts the marketing plan.

Competition is part of marketing because you need to know who is out there and what they're doing—what they're selling, what their price point is, what their unique selling proposition is. Why are they different? When did they start? Who is number one in your industry? Number two or number three?

The worst mistake you could make would be to assume you don't have competition. You have a beverage. Even if it is a niche beverage, there are always other beverage choices out there and people can choose to drink your new age beverage or any other kind of drink.

Even your drink type has categories and subcategories. You might have a sports drink, a tea, an energy drink, energy shot, a soda, or an alcoholic beverage. There are many different products you could have. All of them have competition. And they are all in competition with each other, ultimately.

Let's look at another example. If you have the first organic vodka and you say you have no competition because there is no other organic vodka, you're wrong. There are other vodkas; and because there are, you have competition. Not only that, but there are other kinds of liquor, too.

Or maybe you have an organic soda and because there are not a lot of organic sodas you think you have no competition. Again, you are wrong. There are a lot of sodas, and organic is just one among them. So just being different or having a unique selling proposition doesn't mean you don't have competition.

Now, what can you do to find out about your competition?

You can start by going to the shelves of local markets, clubs, convenience stores, and so on and looking at the products— the products themselves, the sizes, presentation, labels, colors, and evaluate what their positioning statement is. What is their pricing? Are they on sale? All of this information is necessary for you to see who is out there and what they are doing. Learn from them. Learn who is there and what they are doing. Learn from their mistakes. Learn what they are doing that works. Learn what you need to do, or what you could do better.

At the end of the day when it comes to competition you can generalize or be product or category-specific; but realize that either way you are competing for two things—space on the shelf and customer attention.

As far as real estate goes (shelf space), it doesn't matter what your niche or direct competition is. Real estate doesn't grow. These spaces are still the same as they were ten years ago and will still be the same for years to come. You are fighting for the same space in the coolers as all beverages have been all along. You might be fighting soda against soda or specific type to specific type, but it doesn't matter what the other product is, you're competing for a single slot. When it comes down to it you need to convince the retailer that you deserve that space either because your type of product is the next up and coming thing or because your specific flavor, etc., is better than what is there.

Realize, though, that if your products are trying to go in where other products are doing well it will be very difficult to get the space you are looking for. Your competition has your space and they are holding on to the market. So when you go out and shop the shelf, you have to figure out who is in your space and who you need to remove. That is why you need to see how they are succeeding so that you can see how you can fill that need better, and thus make room for yourself.

The other aspect of competition, once you are on the shelf, is the attention of the customer. That customer is going to walk into the store with $X dollars in his pocket and he's thirsty (the biggest motivator in buying beverages), or he is looking for a certain flavor. Now you are fighting for his attention against the drinks next to you. Whether you think you are competing against a similar product or one that is totally unrelated has nothing to do with it—there is only $X to be spent; your competition is now every single product in that cooler. No question about it. You have to have all of your elements strategically aligned to get that dollar.

Impact of Pricing on Competition and Marketing

The next logical consideration to discuss now is pricing—pricing as a competitive factor and pricing as a marketing factor (the two of which are really very related, as you'll see).

Pricing is part of your competition but it is also part of your unique selling proposition. Right now we will focus on this competitive/marketing aspect of pricing, but we will come back to this again in sales and distribution, because pricing goes everywhere with your product—production, shipping, distribution, retail, and consumer. You need to consider different pricing strategies and how each might apply to your drink or range of drink products.

When we start analyzing the price what we are trying to do is set up a price structure that will be convenient on both the side of the consumer and the retail and distribution side. One thing that always needs to be taken into consideration is the gross margin; and again, that is part of the marketing plan.

If you take a look at some of the brands out there, they brand their product by saying that it is very inexpensive to the consumer. Their marketing strategy becomes "we are the every-day, low-price beverage." On the opposite end of that spectrum you have the other guys who position themselves as a premium product. Of course, they obviously don't go to the customer and say "Look how expensive we are!" Their message instead is, "We're setting this product aside because it is superior and worth more of your money."

More importantly, in either of these scenarios, is that you are getting in the face of the distributors and retailers and showing them a product with a certain profit margin. So the strategy in the second scenario is not just about being expensive, it is about the bottom line to profitability. Here you are telling the distributor and retailer, "See that product on your shelf doing a couple of turns per week? I probably won't do that many, but the returns for you will be much greater."

This is a strategy that we've been seeing on the new premium beverages. They are giving everyone a premium mark-up for the product so that less turns are necessary. The product is more exclusive. It's a trading-up phenomenon where consumers are trading-up to get a better product because they can and it feels good, but the real winners are the retailers and distributors. The brands give them more and pump more and more money into marketing; the pricing for the retailer and distributor is great, and they are loving these premium drinks because their burden is lessened and they're not being crunched anymore.

Obviously this strategy cannot work for every beverage, and there is a place in the market for beverages at all price points. But the bottom line is that when you are setting up your pricing you have to remember that you have two buying elements to please—the consumer buyer and the retail/distributor buyer. How you do that is entirely up to you, but we will talk about that in its own place when we talk about setting up price structures later on.

Before we leave this topic entirely, let's take a minute to look at an example of how the pricing for a product might affect how you market to retailers and distributors. We'll use water as an example because it is one that hosts a very wide range of prices for products that are actually very similar.

The price points on water are actually very interesting—they're all over the place. Evaluating the different products, pricing, and placement in a store can tell you a lot about how they are managed and marketed, and tell you a lot about how you will market your product to distributors and retailers.

Let's consider the waters you might see at the average retail supermarket. Let's take your average 24 pack of water. You walk into the supermarket and you see a deal for $3.99 per 24 pack of 16 ounce or half-liter bottles, and there is a full end-cap with about a pallet's worth of these—about 50 to 60 cases; and each of these cases is only selling for $3.99. That means the retailer is probably only making about 15 to 20 points per case. That retailer is not making a lot of money.

Now if you move to the beverage aisle you might see a single bottle of premium water selling for that same $3.99. What does that imply? What does that mean for those products in terms of marketing?

It implies that the producer selling those $3.99 cases of water probably has a broker and is selling direct to the retailer in truckload quantities. It implies that in his marketing plan there is probably only room for a broker and a transportation company—there is no margin to support anyone else. In turn this determines their entire distribution model (which we will talk about in the next chapter).

Now you look at the premium beverages—Fiji Water, for example, that are selling at a margin of a couple dollars per case or even a couple of dollars on the bottle depending on where you are shopping; at that rate they are netting ten times the profit of the producer with the $3.99 cases. That is a product with enough margin to accommodate not only a broker and transporter, but a distributor, importer, and retailer, too. Each of those entities gets their "piece of the pie" and so the product is marked up for each one—at a rate of probably

5% for the broker, 20% for the distributor, and 30-40% for the retailer. There is definitely a lot of margin on a product like that in order to support all involved. This comparison is laid out for you to visualize in the following illustration.

Premium Water Brand vs. Alternative Brand

PREMIUM WATER BRAND	ALTERNATIVE WATER BRAND
Popular 500 ml size Retail Unit Price $1.29 Retail Case $30.00	Popular 500 ml size Retail Unit Price 59-89¢ Retail Case $4.99
Retailer Unit COst Avg 87¢ Case Cost $21.00 Average GM 30% - 35%	Retailer Unit COst Avg 14.5¢ Case Cost $3.00 - $3.99 Average GM 30%
Distributor Unit Cost 58¢ Case Cost $14 Avg GM 25% - 35%	Distributor As you can see there is no room left for a distributor
Manufacturer Costs will vary dependent on different cost factors discussed in prior chapters	Manufacturer Costs will vary but not by too much

Diagram 3.1 – Premium vs. Regular Water Brands

This is not meant to scare you into producing the wrong product, but rather to get you thinking about pricing from a marketing perspective. You need to know that there are many elements involved in the pricing of your product, and that you need to build in the room to accommodate each of them from the very start. Some of those elements could include a

- Broker—perhaps one to help you open accounts, and a separate one to open retail accounts, even another for opening wholesalers for distributors (still taking from your margin, however)
- Employees
- Commissioned sales people
- Distributor
- Retailer

Even if you intend your product to go directly from the warehouse to the retailer you still need to accommodate for the margins for all those elements so that you have the room to grow your product and distribution later. In case you decide that you need to get more distribution you need to make sure your pricing has allocated all those margins for the people you need in the middle. You also need to know that pricing impacts entirely on your marketing plan, and that it is all intertwined. Pricing is essential in your marketing plan!

Positioning the Product

Positioning is another essential part of your marketing plan. To many people, positioning is what the marketing plan is all about—how will you sell your product? How is it different? What is your product's appeal?

As you answer these questions know one thing—the answer is *not* that your product tastes great or that it has a great package. It needs to be something else; something more.

This part of your marketing plan will be your positioning statement; your elevator pitch. What you need to do here is tell the reader very quickly why your product is better. This section is not a complete business plan, it's only a summary. Some of the things you want to tell readers here would be

- Are you part of a very large category?
- Are you part of a small category?
- Are you creating a new category altogether?
- Are you competing based on price? For example, is your positioning statement that you are the lowest priced energy drink?
- Are you competing based on a characteristic? For example, that yours is an organic soda?
- Where will your product sell?
- *What is your positioning?*

It's interesting to see how one thing leads onto or back to another, and again the positioning touches back on your target market—your target market determines your competition, your competition determines pricing, and pricing leads into positioning; and that reflects directly back to that target market. To look at some examples, (again) your positioning might be price-based, or it could be flavors, a unique category, or a new and emerging type of ingredient. For instance we are now seeing the acai fruit as the emerging antioxidant; so now everyone is looking for the next new and greatest antioxidant and trying out others to top that, things like hydrogen.

For all of these the positioning must be very clear so that everything that feeds off it (pricing, market...) works. For instance if you are going to position your product as a high-end product you are going to have to make sure that your pricing structure is aligned. When you shop your competition you need to make sure you position your product at the same level or similar to how they are positioned so that you don't confuse the consumer or the buyer. You want it to be clear that yours is one of the premium beverages that they are shopping for. All of this needs to be communicated in your positioning statement in your marketing plan—so that it is as clear from your plan as from the shelf what market need your product fulfills.

Packaging in Relation to the Marketing Plan

Even though we've thoroughly discussed packaging already in terms of production, we have not talked about it in relation to the marketing plan.

One of the things you have to remember in terms of packaging from a marketing standpoint is that you have different packages for your product and different elements of that packaging that all work to market your product. It's not just about the product itself, you also have the size of the bottle, the quantity of liquid in the bottle, and the type and size of the master case.

For example, you might choose a 6, 8 or 12 ounce can; you might decide on an oversized can or bottle of 16 or 20 ounces that might be packaged in a slick can or normal can. It could be made of glass, plastic, or aluminum. It all depends on your positioning statement and your marketing plan; and that depends on your target market. If you are targeting a high-end consumer and you have a very cheap plastic bottle with very cheap labeling something is wrong with your positioning in relation to the packaging.

Another factor in packaging to consider is that master case. Do you sell your drink in singles? Doubles? Maybe you have a six-pack, or 12 packs, or maybe you only offer your drink by the case. This will depend on where you are selling it, such as in a convenience store versus a supermarket, or if this is a product just for bars and restaurants. You can see here how everything is tying together with positioning, target marketing, pricing, and the essence you want to give your product. Everything has something to do with that essence.

It's all about staying consistent. Again, don't confuse your consumer and don't position your product in a way that does not appeal to them. As an example of this in terms of packaging and marketing we'll take the example of the housewife. Obviously nine times out of ten she is going to buy the product for the entire family. You need to position the product so that it sells that way. That means you have to *package* the product so that it sells easily to her in that way— something convenient for example, like 24 bottle cases, six packs, or something convenient. If it is not something that's very economical you might look at a four-pack; if it's positioned as a sports drink then it needs a sports cap; if it's for children it needs to be spill proof, in re-closable plastics.

All of those factors play a critical role, so once you determine your position and positioning statement you go to your packaging. That packaging has to be 100% in line with that position statement.

If you want to review the mechanics of packaging you can look back to the packaging chapter, but right now we are talking strictly from the marketing standpoint—*What will people think when they see your product?* Do they know what's inside just by looking at it? Look at all the small details like your font and the quality of your plastic. Should your bottle be made of something more eco-friendly like glass or bio-plastic? Or a new material altogether? Is your bottle part of your best-selling proposition? This all has to do with your packaging and it all speaks volumes about your product.

As an aside, but still very much marketing-related, you should keep in mind that packaging is always a perfect excuse to re-launch your product at any time of the year. Now, this is not to say that you can afford to get it wrong in the first place, because your sales will not survive that, but it is to say that packaging is a prime marketing tool with endless potential. But in order for you to be able to do that you have to build that cost into your marketing plan.

In the planning stages, as you are developing your marketing plan, what you need to include here are the numbers—the cost and budget to allow you to revamp and re-launch your packaging based on a chosen time frame. That frame of time might be two, four, or six months…whatever frame of time you think it may be before your product will need that added little marketing push. In terms of the numbers you need to budget for the changes you foresee. You can do this incrementally to ensure you always have something new to offer. To give some examples, you might introduce a new and improved version in four or six months, or start sales with singles, then move up to four-packs, then introduce an eight-pack. You could introduce a new line, a different color or flavor, or take advantage of your sponsorships, like being an exclusive sponsor of the Olympics or a motocross rider, etc. All of these are great ideas that need to be accounted for now.

This is the point where you go back to your spreadsheet and figure in that every two to six months you will need to allocate more money, more time, and more research into packaging. This will make sure you accommodate for those changes in a way that will be consistent with your marketing plan. Again, this adds a layer of costs every four months or so, but it will keep your package fresh and innovative, and keep your consumers coming back to find out what you will come up with next.

To be sure, customers are always looking for something new and innovative, so your packaging plays a critical role in your ongoing expenses. At minimum you will want to make this change and accommodation every six months. If you can keep providing that innovation they will keep buying from you, but when you become old and stale they will look for excitement elsewhere.

Take a look at the list below with some of the changes to one of America's more popular drinks, Gatorade®. Today Gatorade® is still the official drink of the NFL. They have made improvements to their product line over the years. These include all types of changes; label (design, material and colors), container (size, shape and material), closure (size, color, material, shape and functionality) and in some cases with none or very little change to the actual product inside. No doubt you'll recognize many of these, and also recognize the media that came about on each of these changes and therefore their success.

The first batches of Gatorade® came in glass bottles, but it was soon clear that the packaging needed to be as tough as the people who use Gatorade®. Plastic coolers, plastic bottles, and finally powdered drink mixes were developed to help make Gatorade® easier to consume.

- Original came in a 32oz glass bottle with metal closure
- Plastic bottle but same traditional shape
- Introduction of various bottle sizes
- From paper label to plastic label
- Sport caps (various styles over the years)
- New, untraditional flavors
- Catchy flavor names
- More recently you have seen the innovations in the form of Gatorade® ICE, Endurance Formula, Rain, Xtreme, AM, Fierce, Frost and the most recent today is Tiger and G2

We've discussed most of the major points that go into your overall marketing plan. We know we have given you a lot of information, but it is all crucial for a successful new age beverage. However, we are still not quite done.

As we move on to the next few chapters we will continue to discuss elemental parts of your marketing plan. Like those discussed here, these are parts that are both stand-alone elements and integral parts of the overall plan, but in the interest of giving them their due attention we will start to separate out some of these larger and yet unattended issues. We'll start where we've left off here with the Point of Sale and Point of Purchase material.

Chapter 20

....

Marketing: Point of Sale, Promotion & Distribution

We're moving on now to Point of Sale, or Point of Purchase materials. Later in this chapter we will tie this together with promotion. These are a very big part of your marketing efforts, and so are very big parts of your marketing plan. Being the first time that we've really talked about Point of Sale and Point of Purchase (POS and POP) materials and promotions in-depth, we thought to give it just a little more attention by placing it in its own chapter. Along the way, we will, however, continue to discuss POS in terms of the marketing plan as well.

The Purpose of POS and POP

You probably have something of an idea of what POS materials include, although we can venture to guess that it includes more than what you have envisioned. We will detail what these materials are, but before we get to that let's take a minute to clarify the purpose behind using POP or POS materials (do note that these are just two different names for the same basic things, so we'll be using these terms interchangeably).

To be clear, the purpose of POP materials is communication; it is to communicate a specific message. There are two groups to whom you will be using these materials to communicate with.

1. **Consumers.** The first of the groups is your consumer. Most of the focus of POS materials will be towards consumer communication.
2. **Buyers.** The second of the two groups is buyers and category buyers (on the sales and distribution end).

You cannot be out in the field doing all of this communication to get people buying your products, so you need effective POP materials to speak for you. You also need effective materials to speak to category buyers so that they can see how your beverage will reach out to those consumers, and see how you will support them to make sales. To start off, we will focus on that larger audience, the consumer, and talk about how you use POS materials to convey a message to them.

What Are POS Materials?

Now that you understand who you will be communicating with, we can talk about the ways in which you can do that.

There are many, many types of point of sale materials that you might use. These include things like

- Posters
- Price clings
- Racks
- Photos
- Signs
- Pallets
- Stickers
- 3-D cutouts

There are many other things that could fall into this categorization, but what you are basically talking about here is in-store advertising or in-store promotions (those things that are placed at the point where the purchase will be made).

A broader definition of POS might also include the message that is being sent, or the action that is taking place within the store. This could include information/activities such as

- Pricing
- Benefits
- Information and updates
- Sampling
- Special events

In this sense POS would refer more to the message and not to the actual materials that deliver it, but you will see that it is all very much related when we bring this together in the end.

Why POS Works

The real thing to understand about POS materials is their function and potential. POP materials are one of the best communication vehicles to target a consumer right when it matters—at the point in time when they are going to make that final decision and make the buy. It is your last opportunity, your last breath, your last chance to tell the consumer, "Reach for this product!" That is really what POP is used for; it's used to sell. It's your salesman at the store, there for you every day when no one else can be.

Although exterior advertising does certainly have a place, it's the "in-your-face" in-store POS that really proves effective. A lot of people start off with advertising outside the store, without knowing that the best advertising really goes on inside. The reason this is true is that if you get your consumer that close [physically] to the product, whether they are close to deciding to buy it or not, you still have that one last opportunity to say, "Buy me!" And you have a chance to tell them, very succinctly, why he should (because it's what he likes to do). You fulfill the desire of his mood—it feels just right for him to buy your product because your poster, your sticker, all your POS says this product and you should be together. And it is those materials that present you that final opportunity.

To fully understand the impact, you can take a look at the products that do not make effective use of POS materials. As you'll see, there'll be other products on the shelf without POS materials, and the chances are that if that consumer did not come into the store ready to buy that specific product they simply will not buy it. It'll show because these are the products that no one is reaching for, that are doing no turns, and eventually fade from existence in the marketplace, for a lack of effective promotions.

Maintaining In-Demand POS Materials

The demise of un-promoted products shows you the importance of including POS in your marketing plan, and of later ensuring it is effectively implemented. In that interest, there are some things you need to be aware of that will help you as you make decisions about the types of POS you employ; not least of all because this is a cost that can easily become a costly wasted effort if you continue unaware.

One thing you need to keep in mind as you budget, plan, and design your POS materials is that this is one of the things that the competition likes to take down (and to a lesser extent, store personnel as they work to refresh displays). It is easy for them to do that, too. You will regularly have your competitors walking into the store and removing your POS materials as they restock and replace it with their own. You shouldn't let this offend or upset you, because it's how the game is played and it will happen again and again. So your POS is an investment, and it's an ongoing investment. You'll pay for it once and then every time it's taken down (which is at least a couple of times each week) it'll cost you in some way again. At the very least it will cost the time it takes to have it put back up. It may cost you in materials replacement, as well, if the materials are not well-cared for.

This is where design takes on added importance, because if you develop POS materials that are catchy that the retailer likes (the one calling the shots in the store), you'll have an ally on your side. They'll take care of your materials because they are nice, and they add to the atmosphere of the store.

Good POS design goes even further than maintenance, though. If you really create good POS, you also create a demand for it. Take Budweiser, for instance—nice, neon signs are one of their hallmark POS materials, and retailers actually fight to get them. They call up and ask for them without having to be asked to display it at all. Of course, neon signs are a more expensive example, but the same concept applies for more affordable POS materials, too. For example, if you design posters that are in line with the times, that are what's right for the store at the time, that complement the rest of what the retailer is trying to achieve, they will fight for those, too. They'll not only happily display what you give them—and take care of it—but they'll ask you to bring them to them.

Something else to keep in mind is that materials (actual construction materials) can really make the difference. For example, if you have a nice metal sign—something attractive that really stands up—your retailer will help keep that on the shelf (wall, pole...) and keep it looking nice. It's true that will cost you more in the beginning, but it can really payoff in the end. When your POS is just right and retailers like it, you can count on it being there for quite a while. Long story short, don't be afraid to spend a little more on your POS materials, as it can be the very thing that makes them work for you.

Good material design is the place to start, but there is more to know about effectively utilizing POS. First off, we have to remember that everyone is responsible for POS materials (even though you may have to create the incentive to make them share that feeling). This does not only apply to the retailer, though; it also applies to you as manufacturer, of course, and the distributor.

One of your primary responsibilities is to try to make the retailer responsible so that they will put up your specials and promotions, and run the programs you are running with them. But as we said the distributor also bears a responsibility and so you bear one in that respect as well. You will need to train your distributors in your programs and as to how POP materials should be used. A lot of distributors have their own merchandisers, which means that you will need to see to the training of their merchandisers, sales people, or delivery people so they know how to use your POS. You may even do contests with them as an incentive to make sure they follow through.

Ultimately, you are responsible for your POS material. The only way to really make sure it is seeing proper use is to get out there in the field—visit some stores and see what they have. Consider hiring a regional manager in specific territories so they can go into stores and see if your POS is being used, and see first-hand that the material is there and that the message, pricing, and promotion is clear.

A Note about Racks and Displays

One final thing that we would like to add here is a note about racks and displays. We did briefly mention these in our list as possible POP materials, but we should also point out the wider purpose they can sometimes serve.

First off, there are all sorts of these, including disposable cardboard racks, called shippers. These can be very helpful in positioning and identifying the product as it is promoted. They can also help you to avoid slotting fees because they do not take an actual space on a shelf—they are their own shelf-space. Effectively, they present an opportunity to the retailer to bring in a new product and try it out, without losing shelf space to current products (space they may be hesitant or unwilling to give up to a newcomer). Here is a product that comes with its own shelf and promotion, courtesy of the manufacturer. This will often grant you entry into a store as a trial product, giving you the opportunity to prove yourself through sales. Shippers can help get your product in the door, introduce the product, and slide into a store or a region or city with a couple hundred stores without having to change the schematics.

What this should tell you is that POS isn't only always about selling to consumers, it's also about opening accounts. In this way POP plays a critical role in how you get into a store, even if it's only for a trial period. This opens different opportunities—it could be an in-and-out seasonal presence, or it could be your big long-standing ticket in the door. The reality is that POS is not just a consumer tool, it is also a tool that can get you into stores and selling.

Bringing Together the Message and the Material

So we understand what the purpose of POP is, and we know some of the tools and materials that we might be using in that effort. We can begin to look at how this magic happens by looking at some of the applications of it.

Pricing is historically one of the more generic uses of POP materials, but today that trend has moved away from just laying out your price and conveying the message of your product instead. So instead of having huge posters exclaiming your price, you have materials that are more in line with the packaging and positioning of your product. The price may not even be mentioned. Instead you will quite likely have materials with nice, colorful pictures or illustrations of your product that show very clearly what product is being sold and what it is priced for, all reflecting your positioning. To reflect your positioning you might have your sponsored motorcycle or athlete on there (because that's not something that will go on your can, that's something that goes on your billboards, advertisements, and on your POS materials).

Whether you realize it or not, you've seen these types of POS materials a million times. You walk into a store and you see a pole sign, say celebrating Cinco de Mayo or any event with Beverage X. Of course, this could be any type of event, or it could announce a sponsorship, deliver a message, such as the new and improved package, the bigger and better, and on and on. All of these types of materials work as tiny "billboards," if you will, inside the grocery store or the convenience market. Likewise, these can include materials in windows or on doors that consumers see as they come in; before that consumer even walks in the store they're already being told what to buy and how that product identifies with them (because they both like the same kind of music or colors, or the packaging is just right for them).

Budgeting, Financials, and POP

Understanding how to use POP materials is imperative, but we also have to understand their relevance in terms of the master plan—the marketing plan. In addition to what we've already covered, we have to consider POS materials in terms of the financial portion of the marketing plan—the budget.

Before we talk about the numbers, we need to make one thing clear: point of sale materials are not a luxury. They are not optional. They are absolutely necessary, and they absolutely must be budgeted for. In fact, POS materials will be one of the first things that distributors as well as retailers will ask for when you walk in their doors. They will flat-out ask you, "What kind of POS do you have? What kind of POS will you send me?" If you do not have an answer to that question and materials to back it you will not be taken seriously, and you will not get accounts.

What you need to do in preparation for that, then, is to create a POS budget and add it onto your marketing plan and financials. At this point we need to go back to that spreadsheet and add some numbers to the financials column to represent POS efforts and materials.

You'll need to allocate a budget or an amount of POS for every case being sold. The traditional way to figure this is to allocate for every ten cases of product sold; so for every ten cases you sell the distributor/retailer gets X number of pole signs, posters, stickers, signs, and so on for each material you use. If you are spending a lot of money in a particular store or chain you may increase that amount to include larger signs to support money spent on shelf space and end caps.

POP materials will paint a significant part of the picture on your budget spreadsheet. You also need to be aware of, and accommodate for, the fact POS is an ongoing expense, not a one-time expense, and so you need to allocate for POS materials in every month of your budget.

Promotion, Promotion, Promotion

With POS materials covered, we now need to move on to promotion. As you might expect, promotion plays an integral role in the success of your new age beverage.

Promotion actually covers a lot. It is a broad term that covers a broad range of activities to get your product selling. Promotion basically means one thing, and answers one question: How will you sell your product to the consumer?

We've already talked about how to reach distributors and retailers, and we will revisit that in later parts of the book, but the topic we need to address right now is how you will reach your end consumer. For this, there are many tools as well; those include

- Advertising
- POS material
- In-store promotions or sampling events
- Club events (depending on your product)
- Special parties for consumers
- Events near your target market (such as at a school or university)

This gives you an idea of *what* you might do, but you also need to look at the *how* of it.

As you can imagine you need to tie in everything that we have talked about in these last couple of chapters on marketing. You need to tie in,

- Who is your target market?
- Who is your competition?
- What is your pricing?
- What is your positioning statement?
- Your packaging?
- What is your sales and distribution structure?

Everything we covered will have something to do with your promotion because you need to know the basic things like, where your consumer will buy the product, how much they'll pay for it, and why they would want it; that will tell you the type of promotion you need depending on your product, your target market, and your pricing.

This is an exaggerated example to be sure, but if you are doing promotion in jewelry stores and selling products that belong at swap meets then you are doing the wrong types of promotion and wasting your time, effort, and money on something that will never translate into sales.

Again, for which will not be the last time, we are back to considering the target market. If you made a note of your target market before, or if you have one in mind, go back to it now. That target market has led you right to promotions and how you will promote your product. If you have been following along with a spreadsheet, this is the time to take that out again. To the spreadsheet, for events for example (if you are doing events) you would add in,

- How many events you will do per city
- How many cities you will do them in
- How frequently
- How big the events will be

You should also consider the different types of promotions that you might undertake. These could include online promotions, events, or demonstrations. Each one of these needs to be measurable—they need to be budgeted and measured in a way that allows you to see what your associated expenditures will be; you need to know how much money they will cost, for how long, and the frequency of repeating the promotions.

So, for example, if in the first month of launch you did 200 promotions, when you go to open a new territory you can use that as a basis for the next city and the next (perhaps adjusting the number up or down as necessary). Back on your spreadsheet, those promotions need to maintain an ongoing column for expenses. Make no doubt about it, promotions are an investment, but they are ongoing investment, and they never stop. If you stop promoting your products then your competition will step in and take your sales away from you; in this way promotion is, as it always will be, both an initial investment and an ongoing budgetary expense.

Some Final Notes Regarding Promotions

That covers the basics of promotions and what you need to consider in your planning, but there are just a few other notes and pointers we'd like to discuss before we close out the chapter.

First off, do remember that promotions and the promotional plan you devise now will be a very effective tool in opening retail and distribution accounts. While it is true that promotions are primarily a consumer marketing tool, they do also come into play as you start to make your way into these various markets through retailers and distributors.

Your potential retailers and distributors are all very interested in how you plan to sell this product off the shelf. Just as with POS, they want to see that this has been thought through and that there is a solid plan for promotions that is in line with the product and its target market. Whenever you go to visit a distributor or retailer, or an independent retailer or chain, make sure you have a copy of your promotional plan with you so that you can show them step by step,

- How you will help them put the product into the store

- How you will help them sell it off the shelves—by using promotions like events, advertising, PR, and sponsorships

On a related note we'd like to share with you one of our recommendations for new drink developers (all drink developers, really). When you draft the promotion and marketing plan be sure to include pictures so that your product, marketing, and promotion all look very well planned. The way to ensure that it does look well-planned is to show real pictures of your actual events and preparations. This can be things like the tables and cups, the décor, the signage, promoters all in product uniform; it seems like simple details, but it is those details that will give your distributor and retailer the proof that you are not just talking, you have a real, executable, well-scripted presentation that they can rely on, and which will ultimately equate to product selling off the shelf.

Final Measurements

You now know the importance of measuring promotion-related costs, and budgeting for that in measurable ways. Once you start actually executing the plan and hosting promotions and events there is one other form of measurement that you need to attend to—measuring the effects of the event.

What this basically comes down to is this:

- Documenting everything you do for each event
- Testing and tracking

You need to document everything involved with promotions, which each promotion, so that in the event something does not work you will have the information and opportunity to fix and fine-tune your efforts and expenditures. Doing this continually will lead to better and better promotions time after time.

The other side of this is the tracking and testing portion of it. You need to do whatever you can to make the effects of your promotions measurable. Not all effects will be directly measurable, but tracking is very important whenever you can find a way to do it—all the information you gather will have a value, and will be worth the effort to gather it. You want to figure a way to track the success of promotional campaigns and strategies, and, when possible, how much time and money was spent, and how much money or product you sold as a result (such as product sold at the event). Another way to measure the result is to track how many accounts you landed from that particular promotion.

Knowing that you seek to find a measure of your success can actually affect which events and promotions you choose to run, too. For example, one of our favorite events is doing in-store demonstrations because the results are almost instantly measurable and can also include much useful feedback about your product and promotion—information that you can use to further perfect your efforts.

The advantage of in-store demonstrations is that, first off, you are directly up against your competition when you are in the store. Here is that guy again, walking into the store with only a set amount of money to spend, with a decision to make before he reaches the check-out line. He has the product that he's been buying for years, and then he has yours, the newcomer on the scene. He knows nothing about your product—not what it tastes like, smells like, or feels like. He's bargaining and he doesn't know what he's bargaining for. But here you are to promote your product, and you may just be able to sway him.

Moreover, the results of that encounter are measurable. Your demo person will know how much product was on the shelf when they got to that store, and they can tell you before they leave a few hours later how much inventory is left. Those are numbers that will be directly comparable to sales before the promotion; and subsequent sales numbers will tell you if that promotion had a lasting effect after the day-of (if it created a loyal customer who keeps coming back and buying again and again). In addition to sales data, though, that promoter also has a rare opportunity to speak directly with your consumer and collect feedback from the very markets you are trying to target with sales. They can tell you what consumers thought the positives and negatives of the product were, and what elements of promotion do and do not appear to be working as intended, and/or what should be changed the next time around. It is a very simple way to achieve the measurability and results that you need for your promotions to achieve.

This is just one example of how a promotion can work for you, and how you need to measure those results and turn them into effective marketing data. There are other ways, surely, but the end goal is always the same—to help your products sell off the shelves, and find measurable strategies for continuing that momentum.

Distribution Structure in Relation to the Marketing Plan

As we wrap up these two chapters on the marketing plan, we need to take a few moments to touch on the sales and distribution structure. The distribution structure is a topic which we will explore further in the next chapter, but it is also one that is elemental to the marketing plan, and so is a topic that we need to address before we can conclude the discussion on the new age beverage marketing plan.

First of all, we need to say that you absolutely need a distribution model. Like marketing, this is not something you can make up as you go along—it needs to be planned for in advance. You need to have an understanding of what it takes to distribute a product and the different types of distributors and retailers, so that you can decide which is best for your product and target market.

Your specific distribution structure as a whole depends on your product, its pricing, and its weight. Not every distributor will be able to ship a heavy product, or a glass product, or a large product. The costs for shipping will directly affect who you sell to and how you distribute your product. Certain options will be open to some products where others will be closed, and vice versa. If you refer back to those pricing examples we looked at several pages ago, you can learn a bit about how you will set up your sales and distribution structure.

For instance, if you looked at your pricing and figured out that you will need a broker, an importer, and a distributor and retailer, all of these layers will dictate what the distribution structure looks like and what options you have. There are sometimes places where you can skip a level because your distribution structure accommodates for it, because you may be dealing with a retailer who allows you the flexibility of skipping a couple layers. Then, obviously, if your price or product is following a certain distribution structure your sales will be right in line with that. Again, it is the pricing that dictates the sales, and it is the sales that dictate the distribution structure.

If this seems vague and confusing now, do not be alarmed; at this point, with the very limited knowledge you have about sales and distribution, it should be. Distribution is probably one of the single most extensive chapters of this book. This will become much clearer after you read through the next chapter. For now, do know that once you have that information, you need to bring it back here and work it into your marketing plan and your overall business plan. Make sure that you give the decision-making phase of developing the distribution structure its due, so that you can build the most effective and profitable marketing plan for your new age beverage.

On that note, we conclude the chapters on the marketing plan. We'll continue on in the final chapters of the book to teach you all you need to know about developing your distribution plan and sales for your drink.

Chapter 21

....

Evaluating & Developing Your Distribution Plan

We move on now to distribution, where we will thoroughly expand on the topics that we touched upon in the end of the last chapter. This chapter details the essentials that you need to know to develop the best distribution plan for your specific beverage. The end result, that structure, is what you will include in your marketing plan. But first you need to know how to get it there.

In this chapter we talk about everything related to distribution—what distributors really want, the different types of distributors from the small to the regional and very large distributors, including wholesalers, direct store delivery distributors, your own independent distribution, warehouse programs, and all the other many different forms and options for distributing your beverage.

This chapter will focus primarily on the distribution structure itself. In the next chapter, on sales, we will close the loop on distribution and talk about how to actually sell to these distributors, but first we need you to have an understanding of what the various channels of distribution look like so that you'll understand your approach when it does come time to sell. You will come away from this chapter knowing what type of distributors you have available for your particular beverage, where they are, and what the difference between the different tiers of distributors is. We'll explore all possibilities—from the large, big-name beer distributors to the small, unknown wagon-jobbers, and also specialty distributors who sell only to establishments like restaurants and bars. As we do, you'll gain more and more insight into who might be a possible avenue of distribution for you.

That's the chapter in a nutshell, now let's jump right in.

What Distributors Really Want

If you know what distributors really want, if you know how to connect with them and what they are expecting from you, you will make contacts and open accounts far more quickly than someone who walks in and cannot fulfill their needs. As you can imagine, distributors are out for their own business' success first and foremost, so they want to deal with the people who can give them what they really want.

One of the best ways to show you what distributors really want is to first tell you what they do *not* want.

One of the most important things to know is that distributors are not always looking for the best tasting product, or the best looking product with the brightest colors. What they are looking for are innovative products; more importantly what they are looking for are products that sell off the trucks and off the shelves.

Distributors want the product that is continually selling because it is the right product for the right consumer. Distributors want the best selling product! Distributors only care about what your product can do for their bottom line. Is it going to give them five dollars per case, three dollars, two, or 25 cents per case?

Part and parcel to that is knowing how you are going to support that product and sales: support that bottom line (because in distribution, it's always all about the volume moving through the distributor). They want to know: What are you going to do to support sales? Will you come with me and approach all my accounts? Will you open new accounts for me? In the end, that's what distributors really want from you; they really want sales and accounts. If your product delivers that, your product is worth having.

The Role of the Manufacturer (You!)

This is not to say that you can just approach a distributor and they will open their accounts to you. What this means in actuality is that you have to open those accounts, even if they are accounts the distributor is already doing business with (because he is not doing business with them for your product—not yet, not until you open it). This is where the first misconception of distribution and sales lies.

A lot of people think that when you sell a beverage to a distributor it is the job of the distributor to go out and open accounts; that is not true. It is *your* job as the producer to go out and open those accounts.

When you sell a truckload or a pallet of product to a distributor, whether that is a beverage distributor, a wholesaler, or a food distributor that sells beverages along with other products, that distributor is going to buy it and put it in their warehouse. And that's the end of it. Now it's up to you to help the distributor sell that product from the warehouse to the retailer, and then from the retailer to the consumer.

How do you do that?

There is not one answer to this question, there are many. To open accounts for your product and your distributor you have to put people in the field. That may be you or your employees, but someone has to get out there and do things like ride-alongs, where you go out and drive along with the salespeople to their accounts; you need to do direct marketing, where you do telemarketing or mailings to accounts in that distributor's region; you run incentives with the salespeople where you give them a dollar or two per case sold, or ten or fifteen dollars for every account that they open, or perhaps give a bonus when they place a rack, or run contests for a trip or a TV. These are all things you can do to support the distributor and open accounts, and there are more as well. But these are the types of things the distributor wants to see and hear. They want to see that you have a plan for selling your product so they can make money.

Now, this is a long list of ideas and options, given as an example of the types of things distributors really want. This is not to say that you will do every one of these things for every one of your distributors. These plans need to be custom tailored to match your product and your distributors. Your product might not require the bonuses and incentives that you would provide on the retail level; on the other hand, you might find that effort and money is better placed at the distribution level. You might find that certain programs, for instance those that require a lot of sell-through, might require that your program be more aggressive on the retail side than on the distribution side. This is why these different options exist, and you need to choose and develop the plans that are right for your sales and distribution model.

In the next couple of pages you will see some illustrations of a couple of programs that we like to recommend. These, combined with this information, will make it so that you are able to walk into your distributor's warehouse with the programs that are appropriate for the type of distributor you are working with. We will talk about those types of distributors and how to tailor these programs to the right players.

Real Estate Driven Programs

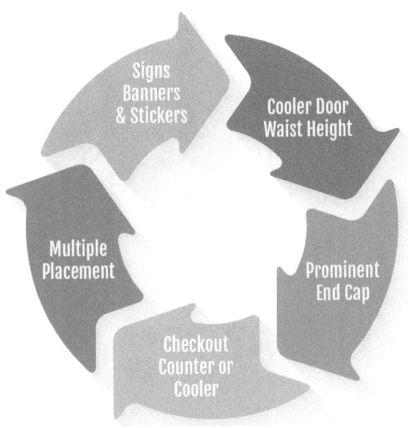

Diagram 3.2 – Real Estate Drive Programs

First rule is "Every program has to be designed to drive sales."

Successful placement means more than just getting an order and a delivery date. It means getting the product placed inside the store in the best possible spots. How do you do this? You do this by providing the best and most aggressive incentive programs to the distributor and his reps when they perform. Every placement gets them perhaps $1 for each case sold during the launch period. They will work for you. The worst that can happen is they don't get placement but you also don't have to pay for lack of performance.

Mix and Match Program for a Single Retailer

Diagram 3.3 – Mix and Match Retail Programs

You can also attach an incentive in any form (cash, vacation, prizes, etc.) to reps achieving the items listed below. Provide incentives for every additional *flavor* that is placed, this will drive more than just the regular product on the shelf. Many retailers have **multiple store locations** but will only try you out at one. Do whatever it takes to get into all of them again by incentivizing. Provide incentives for events; store managers often require vendor support for *special events*, be sure to have a budget for this.

Retailers participate in **retailer ad programs** and are always looking for items to put on special. Be sure to create a calendar with promotional dates far in advance so you can plan together. Specials increase order quantities and if the product sells, well they will reorder.

In-Store Demos get you noticed by the store manager and the consumer and create the communication required between the consumer and the brand and ultimately drive the desired sales.

We just mentioned an instance in which you might want your support programs to be more aggressive on the retail side, but there are instances where that program should be more aggressive on the distribution side, too. If there is a lot of resistance on a new product or a new product category that might require extra space on a shelf or multiple placements in a supermarket then that is a time when you need to put together a plan that is very aggressive on the distribution side because you will need your distributor's people to go out and fight to get more space for you. In that case you want to look at the programs we've just mentioned and illustrated, along with others, and tailor your program specifically to your product. Hence, depending on those elements we talked about in the preceding chapters—positioning, target market, etc.— you will develop support programs that are very product-specific and target specific.

This gives you a good introduction and summary as to what distributors really want; now we need to get a firm grasp on the different types of distribution and the different models of distribution that you have to work with.

Many Types, Shapes, and Sizes of Beverage Distributors

The first thing to know about distributors is that there are many types of distributors and they come in many sizes. There are distributors that specialize in beverage and others that specialize in food but handle some beverages, too; and there are some who sell everything under the sun and that might include beverages as well. Any of these might be a good fit for your product, depending on what that product is.

The major difference between selling beverages and selling other items like candy and snacks is the product size and the weight. That is a very, very large limiter for the distributors, and so a large determining factor in which distributors you can approach. Let us give you an example:

A case of candy might have a very small footprint—maybe six or eight inches by eight inches—and it may weigh one to one and half pounds. A case of beverages might weigh 20 or 30 pounds, and it will be physically much larger than that eight by eight inches. So imagine if you are a distributor and you have a van and that van can carry half a ton in weight (1,000 pounds), and each case of beverage weighs 25 pounds; you cannot carry a lot of beverages in that truck. When you go out selling, if each retailer is buying between 10 and 20 cases, then you can probably only visit one or two retailers before you have to run back to the warehouse to fill up again. That means you are probably getting out to no more than two retailers per day; and for a distributor, that makes no sense.

In the case of wagon-jobbers, you need to consider that they're often selling from the back of a van or the trunk of a car. There's no way they can carry 50 cases; they may not even be able to carry 20, or even 10. So you are limited not only by the distributor's size, but also their vehicles. In addition, you are also limited by their warehouse space.

If a distributor is selling something like snacks or vitamins or pharmaceuticals, for example, chances are you can fit $200 or $300 worth in a corner somewhere—in a spare bedroom or a garage. But if you're selling beverages and your distributors need to buy two or three pallets, they need a warehouse to store it. They can't fit that in a small garage and they can't fit it in a small warehouse because it would take up all their space. It would definitely not be an option for them to order an entire truckload from you, let alone their other suppliers.

What this all amounts to is that there are definite limitations on who your distributors can be.

- The size of the distributor
- The size of their vehicles
- The size of their warehousing

To help you decide what your distribution options are, we'll break these all down into types, in a tier system that we have developed.

Three Tiers of Distribution

The three tiers of distributors is not an industry-wide recognition, it's a division that we created to help our clients and our readers understand the beverage distribution world better. This is to help you understand what types of distributors are out there, and where and what you need in order to penetrate them and get them as your distributor or customer. Very simply, we break distributors down by size into first tier, second tier, and third tier distributors.

First Tier Distributors

At the top of the list are the "first tier distributors" or AAA distributors, the largest distributors in the beverage industry int eh USA. First tier distributors are typically the largest player in your city or town, or maybe even in your state. Often this will be your beer and big-name soda distributors, possibly a Coors, Miller, Budweiser, or Cadbury Schweppes, Coca Cola, or Pepsi Cola distributor. They will have the exclusive rights to those brands for their territory, but they will also take on and distribute other products. The distributors are franchise owners, you're not dealing with Budweiser or the other top brands directly, rather with the owner or manager of the franchise for your city.

These are the best distributors for you or any other product to have, but only if you have the funding behind you. The largest advantage to tier one distributors is that because they have these big names and have to service them at all stores that carry them in their area, they are making frequent stops to all their accounts. You can piggy-back off of that if your product is placed with a tier one distributor, and enjoy the benefit of having your distributor stopping into your accounts several times each week. And not only will your product have the advantage of being delivered two to three times per week, but it also has the opportunity to be merchandised repeatedly each week.

Now, this may make it sound like a simple choice as to whom your distributor should be, but there is more to consider.

First off, it is very difficult to even get in the door to sell a distributor in the first tier. Getting a call into them and getting an appointment to make your pitch is very difficult, because everybody tries to go after the first tier distributors. The thing these producers do not know is this—it is very expensive to work with first tier distributors. Many start-up drink producers simply do not have the funding behind them to start off with first tier distribution (note, that does not mean you cannot come back to them after you have built up your product and sales).

This leads us to the next consideration when targeting tier one distributors in your distribution structure. It usually requires an investment from you to support the first tier distributor—a large investment. For example, a first tier distributor will expect you to go and open two to three hundred accounts, and that costs a lot of money. They will also expect you to spend advertising money in their territory—another large expense. They will expect you to do contests and spiffs, and possibly hire an employee to stay on the premises, perhaps a salesperson or a merchandiser.

All of these might sound like reasonable costs, and they are if you can afford them, but what you need to realize as well is the potential scale of them. For example, a first tier distributor could have anywhere between 10 and 100 sales representatives; that means your expenditures for every sales-related program has to be expanded to accommodate up to 100 people. If those salespeople need samples you are looking at thousands of samples for that distributor, for that territory, alone. All spiffs and contests have to accommodate as many as a hundred salespeople. It's not unusual to see a manufacturer have as many as 10 to 15 representatives working with just one distributor for an entire month just to get the territory account covered.

So there is an advantage and a disadvantage to utilizing tier one distributors. To be sure, if you have the money and the manpower behind you, this is the fastest way to gain entry into the beverage market—it offers the most "feet on the street" and the most guaranteed delivery, but that all comes at a high cost that not all new beverages can afford. If you can, however, it is the way to go.

Second Tier Distributors

Second tier distributors are the medium-sized distributors that may carry just beverages, or they may carry other products as well. They may carry food and beverages, for example. A second-tier distributor may be a consolidator, a master distributor, or a large wholesaler.

Make no mistake, the second tier distributors are still large distributors and still cover a large area. They are only considered second tier because they do not specialize only in beverages as the first tier distributors do. There is still great potential to profit with second-tier distributors, but you must be aware of their greatest downfall.

All in all, the greatest downfall of the second tier distributor is not so unlike that of any other distributor. That is, if you simply gain entry into their distribution or warehouse you are not guaranteed the sale; in fact, it probably won't happen. You still need to make efforts to support your product through your distributor, possibly more so because it is very easy for products to get lost in the crowd of the many various products these distributors sell. These distributors could be carrying anything from candy to pharmaceuticals, to fruit and frozen vegetables. They may have a niche or may not; they quite likely are selling name brands like Coca Cola or Pepsi or Snapple. If all you do is sell product to them it will not rise out of that mix. However, if you go and put a body in their warehouse or out with their sales team they will probably open some accounts for you and generate some sales. The most important thing to know is that if you do not do that, the chances of selling are slim to none.

Overall, second tier distributors can be very profitable and net you great exposure over a territory—if you are prepared to support them in the right way (which you will learn about in the sales chapter).

Third Tier Distributors

The final tier is the third tier distributors. These are very small distributors such as what is known as "wagon-jobbers." These distributors will usually only have one or two vans and sell to 100 or 200 accounts. They normally do not carry an abundance of different products, so you will not likely be competing with a hundred other products the way you might with a tier two distributor, but they also lack the scope and reach that the larger distributors have.

On the other hand, this can work in your interest because what they do have they may be willing to dedicate a lot more time and interest in. This is often helpful for very niche products or boutique-type products, where maybe the focus is less on territory and more on personally serving a few very specific types of clients. They may be key in hitting that niche market. For example, maybe you have a health or natural product and there is one wagon-jobber servicing two or three hundred spas or health centers exclusively for that type of product. That may mean that the third-tier distributor is your only profitable option.

There are some other factors to consider with third-tier distributors, too. For starters, you have to make sure they can handle your product in profitable volumes. A lot of them will not even have the warehouse space to fit beverages. If you can place your product in their warehouse, you will need a very aggressive sale plan to help them sell the product. You may need to build incentives to make the partnership profitable enough for them, or to motivate them to sell your products. These may be spiffs, commissions, or possibly even stock in your company or a beneficial business opportunity, such as helping them finance a larger vehicle and then wrapping it with your marketing. You may also teach them how to sell and open accounts. There are definitely options here, but you do need to be aware that even though they are small and personal, third tier distributors still require a level of support from you, and still at a cost (albeit one that is not extended out to a hundred employees).

This covers the three basic tiers of distributors. That is a start in knowing where to target your product. You cannot simply assume that the biggest is the best, or that the smallest will be good enough. There is more to it than that. Choosing a distributor requires that you look at the specifics of your product and market individually. Once you establish where your product needs to get to then you need to find out who makes those stops. That's how the selection process starts to find the best distributor for your brand.

However, we are not done with distribution yet. Even within these three basic categorizations there are other classifications and programs yet to be discussed.

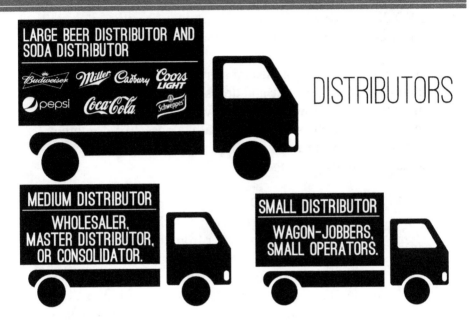

Diagram 3.4- Three Tiers of Beverage Distribution

Classifications of Distributors

All of the distributors that we just went over in the tiers can be further classified into different *types* of distributors. Basically, any of those small, medium, and large distributors can be classified as either a

- Direct Store Delivery, or DSD Distributor, or a
- Wholesaler

Direct Store Delivery

Direct Store Delivery means what you might expect it to; if you are a DSD distributor that basically means that you deliver products directly to the store. For you as drink manufacturer that means that the first, second, or third tier DSD distributor will deliver your product directly to the retail location for every one of your accounts.

However, this does not mean that a DSD just picks up your product at the warehouse and drops it off; they actually do more than that. How much more will depend somewhat on their system; DSD's will have usually a one-, two-, or three-step system. An example of a typical three-step DSD system looks something like this:

1. Order taking. The DSD or their representative will go to the account on a given day (say Monday for example) and take the order from the retailer. They will go into the store, see what was sold in the past week, and then recommend a buy order to the retailer, owner, or store manager. They might recommend that they order 5 cases of soda, 5 cases of water, and other products for say a total of 20 cases of product (one of which we'll suppose will be yours). Then they either enter the order into a wireless device or onto an order sheet and submit it to the warehouse for fulfillment (they may either submit electronically or carry it back to the warehouse themselves). Back at the warehouse, the order is "picked," or placed on the truck for delivery.

2. Delivery. The next step is delivery of the ordered product to the retail location. This is usually within one or two to three days, with one-day delivery being the best. Delivery simply means the product physically arrives at the retailer, where it is then placed in their on-site warehouse.

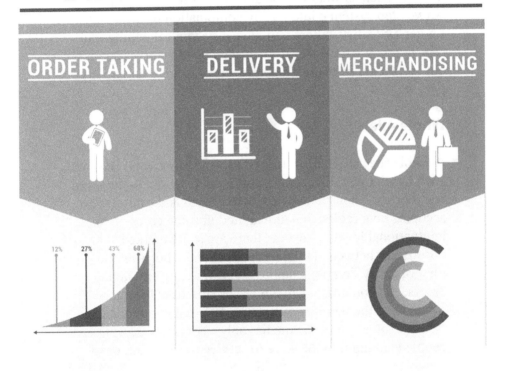

Diagram 3.5 – DSD or Direct Store Delivery

3. Merchandising. The third and final step in the system is merchandising. This is when some employee of the DSD (or the DSD himself, depending on size) goes to the retailer, takes the product out of the warehouse, and stocks it. They will also apply pricing labels and all your POS materials, place racks, etc.

Some DSD's will have a system requiring fewer steps, but the same basic services are provided; you still get the order placement, fulfillment, and merchandising. If that DSD has only a one-step system this may all happen at the same time— they arrive at the store with product on board, inventory and order, then fill the order from the truck or van right then, and merchandise before they leave. That is a classic one step DSD delivery such as what is typical of your small wagon-jobbers. A two-step system could be any combination of these steps. Larger DSD distributors will have a system something like this, but may have a larger sales and delivery force carrying it out (so a team instead of a single representative or delivery person).

Wholesalers

A wholesaler has a much more simplified function. Basically, a wholesaler just delivers product from their site to the retail warehouse. They have a very broad reach and can service accounts on a regional, national, and in some cases on an international level. However there are some marked differences between DSD distributors and wholesalers. First off, they do not go site-to-site evaluating and taking orders. The order is taken either verbally over the phone to someone at the wholesaler's office, or faxed or submitted through some electronic media; only very rarely do you have people walking into the store to service the account, or to provide services such as stocking and merchandising. A few wholesalers will provide these services, but they are additional and come with a fee for each. The advantage is that because they perform fewer services they have lower prices, broader delivery capabilities, and carry a larger line of products.

This is the other major characteristic of a wholesaler—they are not restricted in product to beverage, and they carry a far wider range of products. They do not specialize in beverage, in other words. They also have the ability to consolidate orders so retailers do not have to order 20 cases of beverage they're not ready for; they can order two cases of soda, four of new age beverages, and one of water, along with other needed products like soap, candy, frozen food, or other products, and they will deliver it all at once consolidated into pallets picked and filled for that single retailer.

Who's best?

By now you are probably wondering which of these is the best option to choose; you can probably see advantages to both, and truthfully both do have their advantages. As you might expect, there is no "right" answer to suit all beverage producers. We should point out here that we are not quite done with the different options, either, but we would like to interject that the best type of distributor will depend on your market and placement. This should, however, start to give you an idea of what your distribution structure might look like.

It is also helpful to know that many times emerging drinks use a combination of these, or actually end up starting their own DSD delivery and then using a wholesaler to handle their products outside their local territory as the product grows (we will talk about starting your own distribution shortly).

So which type of distributor is best is still an individual decision, and may not be a single decision. To give you an idea of the best distributors out there, we have included a list on the following page of the Top 10 DSD and Wholesale distributors in each of the tiers. We encourage you to click on those live links and visit these distributors' websites so you can get an idea of the kinds of services each of them can provide for you, and how that might fit into your distribution model.

Top 10 U.S. Beer Wholesalers

Diagram 3.6 – Beer Wholesalers

Other Direct Sale Distribution Options

As we've alluded to, there are still other programs and options that you can choose to use either completely as your distribution model, or in combination with others as a means of covering all territories and targeted retailers.

Warehouse Programs

A warehouse program is something that you develop and negotiate directly with your retailer. This is when you, as manufacturer, deal directly with the retailer, often a large chain retailer such as Wal-Mart, Krogers, or another supermarket chain or a convenience store chain like 7-Eleven, or some other account that you manage directly. The distribution (getting the product from point A to point B after the deal is made) on this will be something separate.

The key to the warehouse program is that you do not need to manage distribution to every retail location. You negotiate and ship only to the chain's warehouse. From there, they have their own distribution that works to service all their stores. The only transport you have to handle is from your warehouse to theirs, and orders are fulfilled from there.

Warehouse programs, as with all programs and distributions, has its advantages and disadvantages; the top advantage being that once you are in with one of these chains you go wide, often nation-wide, in a short period of time ("overnight"—although there is really no such thing as "overnight success" in beverage). The biggest disadvantage is, like all distribution, that getting it to the store warehouse is never enough—you have to get it on the shelves and selling once you've achieved that. There are several ways to do that, though.

The best way to clarify all of this and to show you the advantages and disadvantages, as well as the options to overcome them, is to run you through a typical example of a product that has made it into a warehouse program.

For purposes of illustration, we'll take the example of utilizing a warehouse program with a supermarket chain.

Let's say you want to sell to a supermarket chain that has 500 supermarkets, and they've agreed to take your product (normally they will not agree to take your product if it is new and unproven, or may only agree to try it in a few stores or in a specific region). Now that you have the account, what happens next? How are you going to get your product to the 500 stores?

Now here is the beauty of the warehouse program—you do not have to get your product to 500 different stores. You only need to get it to one warehouse. You do not need to get a distributor, either; they have their own distribution. The supermarket has a warehouse and trucks. All you need to do is ship your product in pallets or truckloads to one warehouse located somewhere in the U.S. and in turn the supermarket will pick it up from their warehouse and deliver it to the 500 stores. They may deliver five cases per store, ten cases, a pallet, or any number, depending on the deal that you made with them.

A bigger concern for you, since distribution is taken care of, is what happens now that the product is in the retail store warehouse (on location). You need to make sure that the product finds its way onto the store's shelves. Often, producers think that is the store manager's job. In theory it is, but in practice that is not the case—not if you want your product to sell and thrive.

In reality, that store manager has a lot of products and only one goal—to make the store money; he does not care which products do that, and you will be competing against other beverages that have full-service DSD distributors; and all of you are fighting for space. In the worst case scenario your product is going to stay in the warehouse and never make it out to the floor, and that's very possible. The most likely scenario is that maybe 10 or 15 bottles or cans will make their way to the floor, but will not have the best location.

What are your options, then?
- Your can hire a merchandising company to help you merchandise your product and ensure it is out on the floor.
- You can do programs with the store managers or district managers to make sure your product gets onto the shelf.
- You can call store managers and offer support, keep your name on their minds, ask them if there is anything you can do for them, answer questions so they know how to merchandise the product properly.
- You can contact (email, mail) the category buyer and do a program with them (a lot of big supermarkets have specific category buyers for beverages, or even specific types of beverages).

These are all real options and there are more, too, but you get the point. The point is that with a warehouse program you have the benefit of a simplified distribution process, but then you need to attack it from the other end, too, to make sure your product sells.

Warehouse programs also work for convenience store chains, but when you sell to convenience stores they don't typically have their own distributor or warehouse. Instead, they will refer you to their preferred distributor. An example of this would be McClain, which is a large distributor that services 7-

Eleven stores. If you sell to 7-Eleven through a warehouse program they will agree to take your product, then instruct you to contact their distributor, McClain, and McClain will service them from there. But as with the large supermarkets, McClain is not a full service distributor (not a DSD), and so you need to also support the convenience store from the other end to make sales, much in the same ways we discussed above.

Drop Shipping

A second option for selling directly to the retailer is through a drop-shipping program. These programs are exactly what they sound like. You are drop shipping directly to every individual one of the retailer's accounts. You pick up your product directly from your manufacturer's warehouse and ship it direct to the retailer. The retailer takes full responsibility for the product after that unless you have some programs in place (and again, we will talk more about what those programs might be when we discuss retail sales methods).

Drop shipping sounds simple and inviting enough, but it is not for all beverages. The costs of shipping exclude many products from utilizing drop shipping as a distribution method. Your price, margins, and cost to manufacture also come into play and impact on the feasibility of running a drop shipping program. To give you an example, if you are working with a $3.99, 24-count case of water, it will cost you about $20 to ship one case from one city to the next. No one will make any money on that product. But if you are producing an energy shot, which is one of the newcomer products on the New Age Beverage scene, a single two ounce unit might be selling for $2.99 retail, perhaps at a cost of $1.49 to the retailer. You can see where if you were shipping 100 of these and making a sale of $149, there's definitely enough margin in all of that for you to pay the shipping from your point to anywhere in the country and still make a decent margin. In that instance, drop-shipping can be quite profitable, and has the potential to become an integral part of your business plan.

Weight of the product will be one of the biggest limitations on drop shipping, because shipping is determined by weight, for the most part. So where a two-ounce energy shot can be shipped affordably, a 20 ounce drink case probably cannot. There are some other determining factors to mention, too. The consistency (physical makeup) of your product and packaging is one. If your product is packaged in very thin cans, for example, they could puncture—something that will not be well-received by anyone involved, and will only serve to anger the shipping company and your retailers. Glass is similarly vulnerable, and also carries the added disadvantage of being very heavy. If you have a smaller can or a tighter non-glass bottle, or again something small like an energy shot, then absolutely drop shipping provides an opportunity to sell and ship directly to your accounts.

Assuming that drop shipping is an option, the next question is, what do you need for a drop shipping program?

There are different options here. You will still need a sales mechanism, even though you probably will not need a travelling sale team. Instead you might have a nice call center to field client calls, and you have an interactive website that has all the programs and literature; you should also have all the electronic media to get all of your information out to the different retailers.

You will not need to include a third-party distributor, but you will need to contract services from a delivery company like UPS or FedEx. There are a few downfalls to consider there, though, as well. Typically those companies drop the product, get it signed for, and you will not usually know where the product ends up; if you're lucky, in a few days or weeks someone will find it in the warehouse and maybe even stock it on the shelves. To combat this, you'll need a plan in place—perhaps one of the sale programs we'll talk about, or some follow-up sales calls to make sure the product is pulled from the warehouse and placed on the floor (or maybe both).

As for actually opening those accounts, there are a few different ways of going about this. Sometimes this comes about because of a client preference. For example, maybe you closed the deal with a chain of stores but the chain doesn't want to do a warehouse program. So they give you a list of addresses for all of their stores and leave it up to you to get the product there. Now you cannot go and hire all the different distributors all around the country to service that account, so you decide to drop-ship the product instead. You do the math and if you can pay the postal service, FedEx, UPS, DHL or someone else to deliver the product then you are in business.

Another way of selling is not through chains but through individual stores, maybe with a direct marketing program that might include telemarketing, direct mail, or direct advertising through one of the trade magazines; these are publications that retailers read, and you can advertise in them with an incentive or a program, such as offering free shipping for purchase of a master case or 3 cases of product, or shipping product with a rack or something similar. The point is that there are a number of options and ways for you to sell directly to retailers, and if you can do that drop-shipping may very well be a very profitable option for you.

Your Own Distribution

Self distribution is an option for each and every beverage producer to consider. In fact, we have many clients come to us looking for help to do exactly this—both produce and distribute their product themselves. Many times these are people who have experience in sales and enough capital to get a few small trucks or vans to get started.

Basically what we are talking about when we refer to setting up your own distribution is you setting yourself up in distribution with the primary intention of distributing what you produce; in other words, buying your own trucks or vans, hiring employees, putting a warehouse together and start selling to retail accounts. Naturally, there are drawbacks and considerations, but this is not something we would try to persuade you away from if you can manage the factors involved. For one, being your own distributor gives you an opportunity to find out what customers have to say about your product—what retailers have to say about it, what consumers are telling them—and it lends itself to becoming a great case study for any product. You wouldn't hear from a distributor across the country telling you what did and didn't work as you will when you are your own distributor. This is a great way to start a business and a great way to build up your own direct store delivery program while ensuring that your product will get the support and attention that it is going to need.

As we said, there are many factors to consider. One of those factors is capital; the cash outlay is significant. However, there are also many investment and borrowing options. In and of itself, the need for capital investment should not be the limiting factor that keeps you from doing this; there are always banks and financing options.

What is more critical to consider is that in order to be efficient as a distributor you need to have a portfolio of products—you cannot survive on distributing your single beverage alone. These do not all have to be your products that you are distributing. Sooner or later making a delivery to a single store with just one SKU, or with just a couple of flavors gets extremely expensive and inefficient. It always a good idea if this is something you are looking at to find a few other items—maybe very lightweight, low-cube items with a high price ticket that will help offset many of the costs associated with making those deliveries. With fuel costs the way they have been, and knowing that they will continue to be a factor on into the future, it is a factor you'll need to consider very seriously to make it as profitable as possible to justify handling your own distribution.

So there are pros and cons to being your own distributor; many of these, however, are more considerations to take under advisement than they are actual positive or negative points. Collectively, those points would be:

- You have 100% control over your distribution and market.
- You have the best possible opportunity to get to know your customers very well.
- You get to know every retailer, store manager, and many if not all of a store's employees.
- You have the chance to speak with employees and end consumers (your target market).
- You most likely live in the area, so are very close to the operation and sales.
- You can easily make special deals, personally.
- You make more money because you cut out the "middleman"—an extra 10, 20, or 30% on the product.
- You need to spend money on infrastructure (warehouse, employees, extra insurance).
- You need to expand your product offerings to make the business viable—either by developing your own portfolio or carrying other manufacturer's products (but not necessarily drinks).
- Your effort is no longer 100% focused on drink manufacture—you now have two businesses to run.
- National distribution would be extremely expensive, and probably unrealistic, on your own.

- You are now responsible for all payment collections (you have to collect money from every single retailer you deal with).
- You get to know key people—such as accounts payable representatives—because you are in close contact and managing your own collections.
- Your representatives and efforts will directly support your retailers and your product, and not middle distributors.
- Your expenditures (investments) become more focused on your products.
- Focus often results in more sell-through.

That's a lot to consider, as anything in business always will be; the one largest consideration, though is as we said—making your distribution efficient so it pays. Not to belabor the point, but if you need to see an example of this you need look no further than the biggest and most successful drink producers of all time—the Coca Cola and PepsiCo's of the world. These are technically self-distributed products. But as we all know, they do not only distribute Coke and Pepsi, they have very extensive portfolios, and they are constantly increasing those portfolios.

They also franchise their business; so even where they do not own 100% of their distribution they franchise out into different cities, states, and countries. There is a lot to be learned by studying the big names, particularly if you are interested in managing your own distribution.

One final thing to understand about starting your own distribution is that it does not need to be the be-all and end-all of your distribution plan. In very many cases developing your own distribution is your avenue into the market, and one that works very effectively if properly managed on the smaller, more local levels. This is also a method that you can combine with other opportunities and selling avenues. You may start on a very small local level with just a van and a small warehouse servicing micro-local accounts. You may extend that by supporting another small or start-up distributor who is looking to develop a portfolio of three or four SKU's. The effect of that will become many small jobbers distributing your product either alongside you or on their own. From there the natural next step becomes entry into wholesalers and warehouse programs, and expanded regional and national sales.

The point is that when you begin with your own successful distribution you plant a seed for your product; you establish a foothold that can thrive and grow from there. When you are ready to approach these large warehouse programs or wholesalers or larger tier distributors you have a lot to back you—you have intimate product and market knowledge, proven sales, effective pricing and positioning, established retailer relationships—a full case study of success that will really pique the interest of anyone whose attention you are trying to attract. Most often, the progression into the larger markets happens naturally, and will lead you through many or all of the tiers of distribution, through the wholesale programs and up to the large tier one distributors. When that happens, and you turn over your accounts and step back from that end of the business, you then net the advantage of their many thousands of accounts that you have yet to tap into.

As you can see, then, starting as your own distribution provider does not mean you will end that way, but by doing so you definitely have an opportunity to rise through the ranks to become a very large and successful new age beverage.

Specialty Distributors

The last type of distributors that we need to talk about are specialty distributors, or specialized distributors. For example, there are some distributors who only sell to bars and restaurants and only sell beverages, or even just alcoholic beverages; there are others who only sell to bars and restaurants and distribute food, but may include beverages; and then there are others who sell only within a niche market, such as those specializing in natural channels or natural food stores.

Taking those examples into consideration, you might go back to your product and see if there is a place where it would fit with a specialized distributor. For example, if you have an all-natural drink with no artificial colors or flavors, or an organic beverage, you might consider specializing with a natural foods distributor and entering the market through natural food stores, vitamin stores, supplement sellers, etc. That might prove the best opportunity for hitting your market target without losing your product identity. Something to note, too, is that you don't need to go out and look for a lot of specialty distributors, as there are only a few that specialize in natural foods channels and they already have a relationship established with the stores you want to get into.

That being said, that does not mean that they are going to do your work for you. It means you have a way of getting your product from point A to point B, but you still, as with any distributor, have to go and support them, help them open accounts, and do all the other work we've already discussed.

One of the other specialized distributors is the food service distributors. These are companies that specialize in selling food, and yes, beverages, too. But they are not beverage specialists—they are food specialists. This might be a big company like Sysco that goes around and services restaurants and bars, selling them absolutely everything they need, from flour to water, to utensils and vegetables…and potentially your beverage, too!

The final specialty is distributors who specialize in bars and restaurants but who are not food service providers; they're what are called "on-premise" distributors. (In beverage when you sell to a bar or restaurant you don't say food service you say on-premise.) These on-premise distributors specialize only in selling to bars and restaurants, and of course that includes hotels and other institutions. A lot of them specialize in alcoholic beverages. Southern Wine and Spirits is one that comes to mind. They go to bars and restaurants and they sell mostly alcohol; not beer, but maybe wine and spirits. They also will sell energy drinks, water, and other nonalcoholic beverages, too, so it's a good avenue of opportunity to approach so that you can get into a lot of these accounts.

The benefit to using these specialty distributors is that many of them are very large. They can still buy locally in one city, but they are national distributors who are in more than one state—they could be in five or ten states or more. Hence, they are a way of achieving rapid distribution.

But, and this probably won't surprise you by now, you cannot forget that just because they carry your beverage does not mean they are going to sell it. These distributors who are not specializing in the mass retail or convenience market, even more so than specialty beverage distributors, require even more support because they carry more products. If you are a food service distributor and are selling everything a restaurant needs you might have 2,000 different products; whereas if you are a beverage distributor, even the large distributors will only have a portfolio of 20 different products. As you can see there is a big difference between 20 and 2,000, so you will need more contests, more spiffs, more commissions, and more people helping to sell to accounts, and more people doing promotions in the bars and restaurants to make sure your product sells.

Classifications of Distributors

Diagram 3.7 – Clasification of Distributors

Summing Up Beverage Distribution

This wraps up all the different options for drink distribution. Understandably that sounds like a lot of different types of distributors but keep in mind that all of those we've just mentioned—food service distributors, alcoholic beverage distributors, natural foods, on-premise—they're all types of distributors that fall under the larger classification of wholesaler or DSD. For instance, the natural foods distributor is a type of wholesaler who could engage in all the different types of programs we just mentioned; and then you have food service and on-premise distributors who are naturally DSD distributors as well. To help clarify this, we have included on the next couple of pages some different matrixes outlining the different kinds of distributors and the classifications they fall under.

You now have the information you need to start constructing your distribution model. There is only one part left to complete the picture and launch your new age beverages—the final piece, the piece it's all about, sales. In the upcoming chapter we will talk about all aspects of sales so that you have that final piece in place, and you will be armed with the knowledge you need to develop and sell your own successful new age beverage.

Chapter 22

....

Selling to Distributors

The chapters on marketing and distribution are about sales, and now we'll continue talking about sales. Instead of exploring and defining distribution channels as in the last chapter we'll focus on the techniques used in selling beverages to distributors.

If you're following a traditional beverage distribution strategy you'll need a distributor in every city or metropolitan area. This means you're partnering up with distributors, they are essential to your business. As one distributor used to tell me: "You marry a distributor".

Selling to Distributors

Your entrance into the world of new age beverage sales starts with distributors. Of course, there is no use in knowing how to sell to distributors if you don't have any to sell to, so we'll touch upon that often asked subject here.

Selling to distributors is very different from selling to consumers. You have far fewer distributors, you can contact them often by phone, mail, email, and you only need a hand full of distributors to be a successful brand. Spend time marketing and selling to distributors. Don't get discouraged if one or two, or ten say NO to you, or NOT NOW. In my experience you can call them back in a few months when you have some traction and try all over again.

Let's talk about how to locate the players, how to approach them, and what you need to provide in order to make the sale. This we will do for each of the three types of players—distributors, retailers, and consumers. In this particular chapter, we will focus on selling to distributors.

Where to Find Distributors

This is the big question for new producers, but it need not be. Distributors are not hard to locate—we deal with them in all tiers on a daily basis. The problem is not finding distributors, it's in selling them on your product. How you go about doing this will depend on your business plan and your budget.

Trade Shows

Starting with the least expensive ways (assuming that to be where most start-up beverages begin), we would have you look to trade shows.

Trade shows are one place where you can begin to make contacts in an industry where you have none. (There are many, many trade shows, but to give you some ideas you could start with one of the largest, which is NACS—the National Association of Convenience Stores, or FMI, or one of many niche trade shows such as those that specialize in natural products). Trade shows are held internationally and locally, regionally, and in different cities and states, as well.

When you attend a trade show you can either purchase a booth space or walk the floor and attempt to make contacts that way. But there is a myth that needs to be dispelled regarding trade shows, which will be essential to understand if you are to benefit from them. One of the most common misconceptions is that you can go to these shows and look for distributors or retailers at their booths; but there are no booths for retailers and distributors; only drink manufacturers have booths. So if you opt to walk the show floor most of the people you will meet are vendors looking for information and product; that may seem like just who you want to meet, but really if you are not buying it will be difficult for you to just walk the show. Still, in the absence of a bigger budget it is a place to start.

To maximize trade shows you need to make those contacts, but you need to do it in a memorable way that provides vendors with information. For that, you need a booth. But even having a booth is not enough to make trade shows worth your while, because if you just sit there and wait for people to approach you it will be a very frustrating trade show and you will only conclude that it is not worth the expense.

However, if you can get vendors to your booth, get the word out about your product and generate some sales, then no matter how much you pay you will think it was cheap. What we would suggest, then, is that you do some work ahead of time (beyond your presentation). Find a list of distributors, email them, call them, fax them; contact them in any way and invite them to your booth. Undertake a direct marketing campaign and entice them to visit you at your booth. You can also do give-aways like free t-shirts or product, or host a "party" complete with invitations; perhaps hold a contest that requires distributors to visit your booth to enter or pick up a prize. Basically, make your presence at the trade show well-known, and get those targets to come to you where you can get your product and your package in front of them.

Direct Marketing

We touched upon direct marketing as a way to introduce yourself and generate trade show traffic; that is really only one small part of direct marketing, though, and only one reason to utilize it.

Direct marketing is also a way to connect with distributors outside when you are not running the trade show circuit. It is as it sounds, contacting distributors through a direct avenue. Our preferred method is telemarketing and phone calls, but you can also direct market through

- Mailing campaigns—this could include postcards, letters, brochures, etc.
- Faxing
- Emailing—do note that you should only use email as a direct marketing method if it is "opt-in"; that is, if the client has signed on through your website, email, etc, to receive emails from you. Otherwise, your emails are considered SPAM. However, if you deliver quality information that clients will want (not just product information, but articles, newsletters, information, etc.) they will opt in to receive more.

All of these methods really can work, but you should also think about the follow-through. It may not be enough to undertake a mailing; you will also want to create an avenue for continued communication.

Referrals

Referrals are an excellent—one of the most valued—ways to locate distributors. As with any referral or "word of mouth," it is always one of the most trustworthy forms of connection.

The beverage industry is really a very small industry. Everybody knows everybody else. It doesn't matter if it is a large Miller distributor, a medium, or small distributor, every one of them has friends in the industry. Therefore, if you sell to one and do a good job of it, they will help you get in with their friends. This works from distributor to retailer and vice versa. Please a distributor, and they will recommend you and your product to retailers. Please a retailer, and they'll be happy to tell their distributors where to find the next great opportunity in beverage. It's not complicated, it's good business sense and it works.

Advertising

Finally, we are left with the staple of all business—advertising. Advertising is not the cheapest method of outreach, but it is an effective one and it can get you noticed.

The place to focus your efforts when you are looking for distributors are the specialty and trade magazines and websites that cater to them. Of course you will have all the choices and options of size, etc., when you place an ad. The most important thing is the placement—find the good trade venues where distributors looking for a product like yours are gathering, and get your name and product in front of them.

The Follow-Up

Once you have made some form of contact and connection, you still have work to do. The most important work lies ahead, and that is the follow-up.

What you want to achieve is visibility for you and your product, but what the distributor wants is to see how you can help them. They want to know where your product might fit into their business. A good plan of action might be to email a sales sheet, and then follow up by mail and send your product information. That should be followed with a phone call to ensure they've received it, and give more product specifications and pricing information.

As we said, though, the distributor wants their needs filled, so start a conversation about their portfolio of beverages and find out where the "holes" are. Distributors regularly lose beverages due to market consolidations, closings, and competition, thus creating a need and an opening for new products like yours. You just have to find out what the need is, and show how you can fill it.

Whatever you do, do not forget about the follow-up. Once you contact a distributor and start talking with their buyer, make sure to send them samples, information, and your distributor package (which we'll talk about soon). Deliver the goods the buyer needs in order to be able to do business with you.

Contracts

Contracts are important for all involved. They are a complicated document, used primarily for the purpose of protection—for your protection as manufacturer, but also for the protection of your distributor. There are several issues that your distribution contract should address, but the most important among them is territory.

Distributors work primarily in a system of territories. Each distributor has an area that they work within, and they will go out and open that certain geographical territory. That costs them a lot in resources and effort; so they need a system of protection so that others cannot just come in and sell to their accounts and undercut that money, time, and effort that has been expended. Distributors want to be contracted with you so that they can be assured that any money and effort put into promoting and selling your product will not be a loss if someone else comes in with a cheaper offer or better options. The most common way to afford that protection is for the distributor to enter into a mutually agreeable contract with you.

Another way that a distributor might be protected is through channel protection, and not geographical protection. In this case, distributors would be broken up by vendor type; one channel might be for supermarket chains, and your contract might restrict your sales through other distributors to supermarkets. Another might be pharmacies and chain stores, and perhaps another hotels and bars, or on-premise accounts. Often you might find that there are two or three distributors in one geographical area, but each serves a different channel. And so to cover the entire territory you might contract with all three of them, with the contracted stipulation that one does not cross into the sales territory (channel) of another.

There are a few other clauses and issues that are commonly addressed in distributor contracts, including:

- **Buy-out Clauses.** Buyout and termination clauses protect distributors from losing contracts. However, sometimes there are instances when a smaller distributor has to yield to a larger one and accept a contract loss. When that happens, they need to see some return on their investment, which comes in the form of a payoff. That payoff may be in the form of sales commissions, buyouts for the amount of product sold over a period of time (such as the last 12 months), a lump sum, or other fair compensation for profits and potential profits lost.

- **Contract Term.** Every contract will be written for a specific period of time for which it is valid. Typically, the original contract will be for a year and will renew automatically; the term can be as long as 5 years with automatic 5 year renewals. Each contract term will be accompanied by certain clauses that determine whether extensions are granted or not. Most often, those are tied to performance, requiring that the performance of the distributor be such that it merits renewal. If the distributor does not meet performance goals then their contract will not renew and will go to another distributor.

- **Trademark or Trade Dress.** Use of trademark or trade dress is an important inclusion in a contract. This is what gives the distributor the legal right to use of your logo, trademark, and dress of the brand so that they can sell and promote you according to your outline. It does occur that distributors sometimes use trade dress in a way not consistent with your marketing plan or message, and so you want to be able to control that. The way that is done is by clearly defining how your trademark can be used and why—how exactly you want your trademark and trade dress to be used in marketing and promotion.

- **Support Programs.** Support and spiff programs should also be addressed in the contract. This serves the dual-fold purpose of providing an incentive and solidifying your commitment to your product and your distributor. In a well-drafted document product support will be a requirement, and will often be tied into distributor performance. For instance, for "x" number of cases sold you (the manufacturer) will invest a certain amount of money into the distributor's marketing plan, or perhaps match their investment. We'll talk more about support in just a bit, when we outline the Distributor Package.

This concludes the major provisions that should be included in a distributor contract. As a last note, you should be aware that not all distributors will require a contract. Primarily, it is the large Tier One distributors who will require contracts for exclusivity and territorial protection; and that's fine, because when you are in with a large distributor you will not need anyone else, so granting them exclusivity for their area is not a problem.

What these distributors are trying to avoid through a contract is diverting. Diverting is when another distributor comes into their territory and undercuts them, thus absorbing the accounts they've worked so hard with you or for you to open. Without a contract diverting does happen, and so a contract will provide your distributor with protection, but also with peace of mind.

Pricing Models

You've reviewed about pricing models in other parts of the book, and we come back to it here briefly. This may seem an unlikely place to address this, but pricing is very important to sales to distributors, as it is what determines their profit, and hence their motivation to sign with you. The pricing model is also important on the side of the retailer, but in some ways to a lesser extent as they really control the price to the end-consumer, so have more direct control over their profit margins.

As we talked about before, you have to build your pricing model prior to launching your product, and well before you start talking to distributors. And also as we said before, you have to leave room in that model for large distributors to turn an attractive profit. This is true even if you are just starting out, and even if you think that you will manage your own distribution; because at the end of the day, your ultimate goal is to go national with your product. That is not a level of distribution that you can manage on your own, and so at some point you will be looking to recruit distributors. Even if you were able to manage to distribute on your own to all the major supermarket chains, you have not gone national; to do that, you need to hit all the hundreds of thousands of independent retailers, pharmacies, convenience stores (chains and independents), and in order to get those accounts you will have to deal with distributors, and you will need the margin to pay them.

So regardless of what point you are at today, you need to take into consideration all the different levels of pricing that will ultimately be required. Let's look at a typical scenario and then layout the levels of pricing that you need to build into your model.

Many small startups enter the market with local accounts to stores in their own backyard. The temptation here is that, because there are no other levels involved, they only need to make 30 or 40% to keep their drink alive, and they price to accommodate a 30 to 40% margin for themselves. In reality, if you are distributing your own product, you should be making up to 70 to 80% margin. But selling for less and being more affordable is all too appealing, and so they fall victim to that temptation. After all, if you were selling through a distributor you wouldn't be making that money. And the consumer loves an inexpensive product, don't they?

That may be true, but those kinds of decisions will always come back to haunt you; because come next quarter or next year, you are too big for yourself, and you need a distributor. And when you approach that distributor, he is going to want his margin, which will be in the area of 20 to 35%. If you are only making that yourself, or only 5% above it, there is nothing left for you, and worse, nothing left for the product support that will be necessary to carry your product through larger markets. Even if you toy with expanding your own distribution, you'll soon find how impossible that is, because you do not have the margin for transportation, hiring a co-packer, and supporting the retailer. By not writing in the margin for distribution now, you will destine your product to forever be restricted to your immediate area.

To wrap up this discussion on pricing models, let's try to give you an idea of the margins you need to consider.

- **Distributors.** The margin for your distributor will depend on the size of the distributor and your product, but eventually to access tier one distributors you will need a minimum of a 20 to 25% margin, and upwards to 35 or 40%. The industry standard set by the top three tier one distributors is 30%.

- **Retailers.** As we said, it's hard to pinpoint margins for retailers, because each retailer will set their own price. For chains and franchises, the price will remain consistent for the chain. What you will have to do is negotiate with the retailer to find out what their expected margin is, and what their pricing will be. You can start off with your suggested retail price with a margin of 30 to 40% built into it for the retailer, which they may accept or decline, and whatever number you land on with them will determine their profit margin.

- **Brokers.** Brokers are one of the more overlooked entities in pricing models. We'll talk about brokers in the next chapter, but for our purposes here you will want to include a margin so that they remain an open option to you; for that you can count on a figure between 2 to 5%, and possibly as high as 10% if you are dealing with a strong, aggressive brokering company.

Of course, added to these factors will be the other necessary items and margins needed to support your product. Those need to be accounted for, too, as well as a level of profit for you. One of the best ways to do this is to start on the consumer side, look at your product, and determine a price that can work. Then you start calculating, taking away these margins for all the necessary levels and players. Here is where you may need to adjust that price model. What is left becomes your margin for support programs, which is no less important. If the numbers do not add up and leave enough profitability for you or for your support programs, you'll need to make adjustments again.

When you find the right price model that makes sense for everybody you will be able to recruit the distributors, because they can see that your business model makes sense and has profitable potential. The price model lends itself to every little segment of your business, including, not least of all, sales. It is what determines whether or not you can go to those trade shows, afford to direct market, advertise in the trade magazines, and whether you'll land the referrals because of your solid model and great, profitable margins.

Support

Something that is very important to distributors is support—how you will support them so that they can promote your brand and establish and grow your sales.

There are a number of things that you can do that support your drink and your distributor. Whichever of these you choose, you will need to include it, in detail, as part of the distributor package. Some of the support that may be needed includes:

- A representative in their territory who does things like doing ride-alongs in delivery trucks, opens accounts, visit stores
- A mailer sent out to all the retail stores in the territory
- Point of sale material—posters, stickers
- Samples and sampling
- Merchandising
- Support programs (spiffs, commissions, etc.)

The "little things" are also a means of distributor support—throw parties for them, stay visible by giving out freebies like logoed pens, t-shirts, briefcases, and so on. These aren't the things that you'll include in your distributor package, but they are small tokens of support that build relationships and keep your presence and support known.

Some of the other methods of support are not 100% the responsibility of the manufacturer. There are support systems that you can put into place that guarantee that all or a percentage of the money you invest in support will be matched by the distributor. These can apply to co-op programs or co-op events, sponsorships, or mass-media marketing. Cooperative support programs can also be things like slotting.

In basic terms, co-op support programs ensure that the distributor will make an equal effort to yours, and provide an incentive for them to do so. It's very easy for a distributor to ask you to spend money sponsoring events and advertising, but when they realize that they, too, will have to invest in the program, they will be more discerning and take more care to choose profitable marketing avenues. So there are two ways to look at co-op programs; one the one hand, as part of your distributor package they say, "I'm willing to help you bear the cost of marketing," and on the other they give you some security, too.

This list is just a start in terms of support. The bottom line is that if you keep in mind that you *do need* to support them, that you bear that ultimate responsibility for sales, you will be more than halfway there.

The Distributor Package

We've mentioned the Distributor Package a number of times now, and this is something that ties in directly with distributor support. All of those major items of support need to be included and communicated in your distributor package.

The distributor package is the actual "sales pitch" that you give to the distributor. It is your personalized sales proposal specifically designed to show them how you will support them, and sell them through your efforts.

A distributor package can include many things, and each one will be a little (or a lot) different, because it will be tailored to your product and your business plan. There are some basics that should be included in every one, though.

- **Spiffs and Commissions.** Distributors like to see you supporting and motivating their sales people and sales managers, because they know that that is how they make money. So although spiffs/commissions are targeted directly to the sales team, they are very enticing to distributors. These are the programs that reward each seller or manager with a percentage of the sales, or a set amount per case sold. For example, each salesperson may get fifty cents, $1, or $2 per case of product sold; or $15 to $20 for each rack placed at a retailer. You may reward them with $50 for opening a new account, or $X for selling more than 100 cases in a week. You can design the program however you choose, and it is a definite inclusion in your distributor package.

- **Point of Sale Material.** You'll already have this planned, you just need to include it here so the distributor can familiarize with it. For this section, you will want to include things like stickers, sales sheets, posters, pole signs, photos of events you've done, press releases and/or media coverage, renders of photos of your product, product specifications (how many items per case, bar codes for the case and the product, cases per pallet, pallets per truckload). Anything and everything that sells your product will sell your distributor.

- **Contests.** Contests are similar to spiffs and commissions in that they are targeted to the sales force more than the distributor, with the key difference being that there is only one or a few winners. Whereas with commissions everyone who sells wins, with contests they need to compete to win. Often the prize will be something like a trip with their spouse or their family, or an electronic device, a TV…the reward should be sizable and enticing, though, or no one will bother with the added effort. Like spiffs, you can design your own version; the contest could be to be the top seller, or could be a drawing-type where anyone who sells more than 100 cases is entered into the drawing for a new TV, and so on. There are many, many possibilities for contests.

These are the basic types of things that should go into your distributor package, but let's talk just a little about the physical format of it.

Ideally what you should do is arrange all of this very nicely in a quality folder with your logo on it. All of your sales sheets, press releases, POS materials, specifications and everything else will be inside, including a business card and prominent contact information, thus creating one complete, concise presentation that largely speaks for itself.

A Step Further

As we all know, it is often the added effort that sets you apart from the crowd, and that is just what you want to do in order to sell your distributors. So while a basic distributor package will get you in the door and get you some attention, a more informative one will put you on the top of the pile.

If you really want to impress potential distributors, use it to tell them exactly what you will do to open accounts for them. This is the thing that separates the small guys from serious players, and it is what will show that you know your stuff and are serious about successfully selling your drink.

This part of the package does not need to be overly long. A succinct marketing plan will suffice. In it, lay out exactly how you will go out and sell the product from their warehouse to their retailers. If you do that, yours will be the best distributor package they've seen. This is our strategy, and it has been proven time and again. In point of fact, we have actually received calls from distributors who have dealt with specific products and really liked them, but who could not sign them for their lack of a sales and distribution plan and impressive package. They call us and ask us to take a look at these brands and work with them just to develop a saleable plan.

The one thing to remember above all else with your distributor package is that it has to have some meat to it. It cannot be just for show, and it needs to go much further in depth than "here's my product, please sell it." It has to be the means to that end. Something to always keep in mind is that, given the high valuations of the market today and how "hot" the industry is, there are lots of people jumping in and developing new age beverages; distributors are fielding three to five calls every day, and when you approach them you have to be different— and prepared!

Finally, limit your outreach to what you can handle, and what you are funded for. If you do not have a lot of funding, start on a smaller, more localized level and build sales and revenue from there. If you are well-funded you can approach several distributors at the same time; but if you are operating on a smaller budget, then only approach one or two. Don't just blanket all the distributors you can find, because if you get lucky and they sign with you, you don't have the money to follow through with product support or delivery. Remember, all of your efforts have to be duplicated for every distributor, which duplicates your costs as well.

Create Your Budget

On that note, we'll wrap up this chapter on selling to distributors with a section on budgeting to support those efforts.

For all of the support programs that go into the distributor package, you need to create a budget—before they are implemented, so that they are accounted for and funded. You cannot just take opportunities as they come along; you have to plan for them so that you can attend to all expenses and facets of product support, production, and sales. What you most need to know ahead of time is, how much will you allocate per city, or per distributor, or per case? If you do not know this, you will quickly lose control of your funding.

Let's look at an example.

Let's say you allocate 30% of sales back to the distributor. That means that 30% of the sales made by distributor A will be allotted to fund *that distributor's* marketing and support. If you sell $18,000 worth of product to distributor A in a month, $9,000 will go into marketing and support for distributor A. Working together, you and distributor A will decide where that money should go—such as into events, advertising, or sponsorships, etc.

Of course, you cannot expect (although many new manufacturers do make this mistake) that your sales will fund 100% of your marketing budget. When it comes time to open a new territory, you will need to invest money that is not yet being reflected in that area's sales. For instance, you may spend $100,000 to open a new market, and that money will not come from your ongoing budget, it will be money that is invested from other funding. It's a hard dollar figure that you are committed to, and you need to know where it is coming from. Likely the answer is profits from another region, and in time the money you make in the new territory will fund your next level of sales, and so on. Still, it is a real amount, and not a percentage of sale revenues.

When you do create your budget, you need to be conscious of all expenses. Many times manufacturers budget for the big expenses, but forget that everything they send out has a cost; so not only are you budgeting in the big things like spiffs and commissions and advertising, but also the little things like t-shirts, stickers, and posters. It is very important to identify all of these line items, allocate a figure to it, and make sure that it is in either the launch budget or the ongoing budget.

Unfortunately, much as our readers would like one, and much as we'd love to give you one, there is no solid figure to say how much money will be needed to fund this budget. Your budget will depend on your drink, your production costs, the type of company you have, and what you want to achieve, as well as the distributor that you want to contract. It will cost you more money to go after the tier one distributors, whereas a smaller distributor can be supported with less funding (but of course, we've already talked about the difference in sales potential).

To put something of a figure to it, we can go back to that figure of 30%. The big three distributors have made this something of an industry standard, at least for the tier one distributors. That's a good rule of thumb to start with as you begin to take a look at your numbers and funding. Again, this is for your ongoing budget, though, and does not reflect the costs of launch and opening new territories.

This ends our chapter on selling to distributors. The next logical step is to sell to retailers, and then on to consumers. This will be the subject of the final chapter of our book, as we complete the path from production to sales to the end consumer.

Chapter 23

....

Selling to
Retailers & Consumers

This is the final chapter of our book, but no less important than any of the others. This is the chapter where we finalize our sales with selling to retailers, and then on to our ultimate target market, the end consumer. Along the way we'll also stop by the broker's realm to discuss the role of the beverage broker, and how you can potentially benefit from that relationship. We know you are anxious to move on with your project, and so we'll jump right into selling to retailers.

Selling to Retailers

There is a great variety of different types of retailers, and how you sell to each one will differ, too. We are going to break the types of retailers down into categories much as we did with distributors, so that it will be easier to see the sales strategy that you will need to service each one.

To begin with, let's outline the different types of retailers. They are

- Supermarkets—which can be further broken down into independent and chained supermarkets
- Pharmacies—again, both independent and chained pharmacies
- Club stores—such as Sam's Club or Costco
- Convenience stores (or "c-stores")—these can be independent or chained stores, and the category also includes places like gas stations and liquor stores
- On-premise—hotels, bars, restaurants
- Institutional accounts—large kitchens such as those in schools, colleges and universities, or government buildings
- Vending—a combination of a distributor and retailer account, as the one will serve both functions
- International—export outside the U.S., with Mexico being one of the major markets for U.S. beverages (Many of you already know that we created the largest export group into Mexico, the Mexico Sales Alliance, which does business with every single account in Mexico).

Now that we have identified the players, let's talk about your game strategy for each of them.

First off, if you sell to distributors they will have retail accounts already; that does not automatically mean you have "sold" those retailers, you still have to work to open those accounts. You do this by

1. Building a margin into your price model so that distributors can profit from the resale, and
2. Supporting the brand and personally opening accounts

We know these two basics well by now; the question we are left with is, how do you reach retailers through your distributor? We'll go through the different categories separately to find the variety of answers to that question.

Selling to Independent Retailers

A given distributor will have many different independent accounts, across all types. These will include independent c-stores, supermarkets, clubs, restaurants, and bars. Each one will have basically one decision-maker. That may be the owner or a manager, but they have the final say over what products are in and what's not.

One way or another, this person needs to be reached and convinced that your product is a good product for their clientele. If the distributor doesn't do that, then it's up to you. You will want to approach this retailer personally, either by telemarketing, visiting them, or direct mailing (or a combination) and open the account yourself (or through one of your representatives). When it comes down to it, opening independent retailers is very simple—you just have to go out and present your product, and sell it. Simple doesn't mean easy, though, because this is an effort that will have to be repeated many times for each independent retailer.

Selling to Retail Chains

Chains can mean the large, well-known regional or national retail chains like 7-Eleven, Circle K, Kroger, Walgreens, or Wal-Mart, or it can refer to small chains where a single owner may own somewhere from two to 20 stores. Regardless, you sell to each of these in the same way.

With chained retailers your target is the buyer. This may be a category buyer who buys all beverages, or it may be a buyer who buys all of the products sold in the stores. In some cases, the buyer may even be the chain's owner. What you need to do is to present yourself to this buyer (either alone or with your distributor), sell them on the product, and then let the distributor take over from there. Of course this is an oversimplification of this process, but that is the basic method of selling to chained accounts with a distributor. Each chain, though, will have their own buying patterns. Some are centralized, while some are regionalized, and some have district structures. You may deal with one buyer for an entire chain, or several across all the territories that you are selling within.

For example, Walgreens breaks their chain into districts, with each district having around 30 stores. Additionally, they have special managers who are allowed to buy for about five stores. This structure actually opens more opportunity for you to sell to the Walgreens chain, though. A worst-case scenario might be that you present to the corporate office, controlling about 6,000 Walgreens stores, and are declined. So then you approach each of their 200-300 district managers and sell them one at a time. If that fails, you can go to the local buyers who control five to ten stores. If you are still not making sales, you can resort to approaching each individual store manager. This may sound like an act in futility, but we have done just this with success. It's not the easiest sales route for a retail chain, but it can produce results in the end.

The very basic method of selling to chained accounts, then, is to locate the buyers responsible for the stores you want to be in, and start selling on down the line.

Selling to On-Premise Retail Accounts

The other entity to address in regards to retail sales through distributors is on-premise accounts. This is another case where you will need to do a lot of personal selling and/or selling alongside your distributor. The way it works for these types of retailers is that the distributors will regularly sit down with them, with a buyer, the chef, or bar manager, present products, and do product samplings. You will need to either accompany them yourself, or with a representative, or at the very least provide the samples and information they need to make the presentation. For these accounts, it is really necessary to maintain contact because both the retailer and distributor are dealing with hundreds of different products, and it is very easy to get lost in the crowd. Thus, the personal approach—visits, contact, ride-alongs, etc—take on greater importance.

Selling to Retailers through Buying Clubs

Finally, you also have the option of selling to retailers through your distributor through buying clubs.

A lot of convenience stores, supermarkets, and independents belong to a retail club. Membership in the club gives them buying power in the form of discounts, bonuses, and specials. To reach these retailers, you would need to approach the buying club, present and sell to the club and then service through your distributor as with the other retailers. This gives you access to between 100 and 1,000 retailers through a single club, with only having to sell to one buyer.

Selling to Retailers without Distributors

You can also sell to retailers without working through a distributor, through the warehouse programs that we discussed before. To recap, this is where you sell to a chain, usually a big-box store or large chain, directly through their buyer. The procedure here is to approach the beverage category buyer, which will be the one person who makes the decision for all of the stores. This is somewhat similar to the process for selling to retail chains and clubs, in that you sell to only one representative but access hundreds of stores; only in this instance you are on your own without a distributor beside you. When you do make the sale, it will be large—truckloads at a time, and only one delivery point to manage.

Something to be aware of, in addition to the pros and cons outlined before, is the payment contract. Different warehousing programs may attempt to contract their purchases through a scan program. This means that instead of a straight sale and payment in 30 to 90 days, you only get paid when a product is scanned—basically a consignment arrangement. So instead of receiving payment in a month or two, you may not be paid for four months or more, and if the product doesn't sell they can return it and have lost nothing; you will be the only loser. If at all possible, you want to avoid scan programs at all costs.

Warehouse programs are also a possibility for chained convenience stores like 7-Eleven and Circle K. That is not something that you will hear directly from the retailer unless really pushed, because they really want the free labor that a DSD or distributor provides; but it can be done. The basic process is to sell to corporate and arrange for delivery to their warehouse or distributor. Again, personally presenting and selling your product to them. But there are certain criteria your product will have to meet, based on the weight of your product. If your product exceeds the formulation, no matter how good a retailer package you have it will not be considered for a warehouse program.

There is a catch to successfully selling convenience stores this way, and that is this—you *must* have a *killer*—and we do mean *killer*—plan to sell it off the shelves; in other words, a *killer* retail package. Along with funding (because you must be able to turn revenue to continue to produce large orders for these warehouse programs), a stellar retail package is the requirement for even considering sales to c-stores through warehouse programs. With that in place, though, it can be done, and has been, despite what you may have heard otherwise.

One final point to mention, since we're talking here about selling direct to retailers without distributors, is utilizing drop-shipping as a means of selling to retailers. We've already gone through drop-shipping in detail, so we won't go through it all again here, but this method of selling to retailers should be included on the list. You'll recall that this has certain criteria and requirements attached—your product will need to be smaller and lighter so that it can ship affordably, and you will have to maintain the sales team to open accounts. The process for doing that will require that you and/or your sales representatives contact the designated buyers, either on a corporate or singular store level, present and make the sale, then ship the product through a third-party company like UPS or FedEx.

This tells you how to approach each of the different types of retailers, but as with distributors, there is one essential piece that you will need, no matter who is doing the selling or what type of retailer you are selling to. That is the retailer package.

The Retailer Package

The retailer package is fundamentally the same as the distributor package; it is the presented plan for support and marketing that speaks to the retailer to show them how your product will be sold and how you will support the retailer.

The retail package can actually be a physical document, just as the distributor package can be. It can be a brochure, a binder, it can have multi-media (a CD, audio or video); it can also contain photographs and text. However you choose to present it, this is your plan that tells the retailer what they want to hear—how you will help them sell your product.

Like the distributor package, there are some basic things that you will want to be sure are included in your retailer package, and then you can customize and add to it from there.

- **Sampling & In-store Promotions.** Sampling and in-store promotions are primarily a marketing tool used in grocery stores or supermarkets, or the larger retailers and club stores. To recap a bit, these are the events that take place on-site, where a trained representative presents your product to the consumers in a store and offers free samples; they also do things like monitor store inventory before and after the event and collect feedback from consumers. You will need to plan in advance for samplings and in-store promotions, and include them in your retailer plan as a show of support. At first this may be very basic, but over time with a few events behind you, you can communicate more about your plans and also include photos and summaries of your typical promotions.

  In-store promotions also encompass sales specials and programs (such as buy one get one free specials, special pricing, etc.). These are ideal to couple with a sampling event. You should plan ahead for these, too, and also present them in your retailer package.

- **Merchandising.** Merchandising we've talked about in a few different places before. This is where you have someone—a representative or your full-service DSD distributor—go into the store, stocking shelves, and placing promotional posters, stickers, and other point of sale material. It is very important to include this in your retailer package for two reasons; one, to communicate to the retailer how the product will be promoted in-store, and two, to outline who is responsible for attending to that.

  Incentives to the merchandising team may also be included here (and should be if you are in fact doing them). Just like with salespeople, you can run contests and reward programs for merchandisers, where perhaps any team that places an end-cap or a side-stack or gets additional placements in the store earns maybe $2 per case for the placement. This drives sales in a couple of different ways, because these require more product, and so result in more cases purchased by the retailer, and also gets product on the floor where it is more accessible (not hidden in the warehouse). Extra placements also provide new opportunities for merchandising.

- **Pricing Specials.** Pricing specials are just what they sound like—specialty prices for a limited time designed to drive sales. Your traditional pricing special would be a buy one get one free or a lowered sale price. These are primarily targeted to the retailer as a way to get them to take on more inventory. They are not as consumer-focused as they might appear (because we really do not want to do anything to cheapen your product—we want to keep you as close to your suggested retail price as possible for the sake of reputation and value). Pricing specials are, more than anything else, a tool to get product on the shelf in large volumes. They are a part of your retailer package that shows them what tools, what means, you are going to give them to do that.

- **Distribution Options.** Remember, your retailer package is a comprehensive account of all that the retailer needs to know in order to feel confident that you can deliver the goods and help them make sales. Retailers know that the distribution of product is elemental to that. So one of the first questions they will want answered is how your product is going to reach them, and whether that is a reliable plan. This needs to be laid out in the retailer package, too. You need to include all the options for distribution so that each retailer can find the solution that is suitable for them. This shows, also, that you have covered every aspect from production to sales and have a solid business plan to support the product.

- **Point of Sale Material.** We know what this is, and so you know that Point of Sale Material means the most to the retailer, above all the other entities you might deal with. Every retailer will be expecting to see POS material included in your plan. You need to have all of this "sales collateral" ready and done when you walk into a retailer to open their account. You need to list the various POS that you will provide, show photographs of it, and provide samples and examples. The retailer needs to know that the physical materials they need are in place, and will be there for them.

  This is also the place to think about other promotional items (like lighters, t-shirts, pens, and other gadgets) even though they are less point of purchase and more for general promotion and promotion to the retailer. This isn't necessarily something to lay out in the retailer package, but something to include along with it to keep you fresh in the minds of those you need to sell the most.

- **Rack Programs.** A rack program is pretty much in line with point of sale and point of purchase. They are an added tool to get shelf space and move inventory from the warehouse to the consumer. These are a better alternative to slotting programs because they do not take up fixed shelf space, and do not come with the fees that slotting does.

  Rack programs are where you provide a movable rack to be placed and stocked with your product, thereby creating your own shelf space. These require a larger investment, and do have some drawbacks (mainly, they are costly and require upkeep and care so they do not get lost in the warehouse or taken by owners or managers); rack programs are not a good idea if you do not have a DSD arrangement with a representative looking after them on your behalf. An alternative to racks is cardboard shippers, which cost about 90% less than racks at around $10 to $15 (of course they have 90% of the lifespan, too, but are an easier loss).

If rack programs are in your budget and marketing plan, they should definitely be in your retailer package. This gives your retailer options and avenues, especially for those with more limited space and a full line of beverages in place.

- **Contests.** As with distributors, retailers enjoy a good contest, too. For retailers, these are usually held between chained stores or within regions or divisions. There is a lot of communication that goes on between stores in a chain and there is always a lot of competition to prove their worth in the greater scheme of the company. You can capitalize on this by running contests for things like the top-selling store, the store to sell the most through a promotional campaign, or the store with the heaviest sales volume for a time. You will need some enticing prizes (one thing that works well is electronics, like giving an iPod or five iPods to the top store). Having contests in your retailer package provides more of a show of support for them directly, and capitalizes on that age old question, "What's in it for me?"

Contests can be accomplished for independent stores, too, although you'll need to be a little more resourceful. You will need to run the contest through their cooperative or a similar organization to get enough stores involved to make it a true competition that raises sales.

- **Advertising to Drive Traffic.** Retailers do not need you to tell them that advertising drives sales, but they do need to know that you understand this and that you understand it to be your responsibility, and not theirs. Retailers will be looking for your plans for accomplishing two things—to drive traffic to the store to get your product and to sell once the buyer is in the store (which was covered by POS materials and promotions). This part of your plan will focus on the outside advertising that brings people into those retailers who carry your product. These are things like co-op advertising (in mailers and flyers), frequent shopper discounts (additional discounts to loyal shoppers in that store—contrary to popular belief, these are funded through product/producer support and not through the retailer).

  Advertising to drive traffic to the store is an essential component to your retailer package; it is not optional. The retailers will choose your product over others if they see that you have a plan to sell it off the shelf. They expect to see that you have accounted for advertising in the form of print, radio, outdoor advertising, TV, vehicle wraps, sponsorships, or events.

That wraps up the basic retailer package, and wraps up selling to retailers. This should give you a good foothold on how you will get those managers and store owners to accept your product and sell it through to the consumer. That is a subject that needs addressing, too, but before we have that final discussion we want to tell you a bit about working with brokers, and how they can fit into the sales game for sales to retailers and distributors.

What are Brokers and Where Do They Fit In?

A lot of producers don't really have a clear understanding of what a broker is, or what their potential role is in promoting sales of new age beverages. Brokers are a big part of the industry, though, and something you should know about.

A broker is many things, but primarily brokers are groups of people that specialize in representing other people's brands. They are a big part of sales in the beverage business; some companies rely exclusively on brokers to get their product sold. You can basically think of a broker as an outside sales agent, but there are limits to their responsibilities.

First off, let's talk about what a broker is not. A broker is not an employee. Therefore, you do not have to pay workman's compensation or other benefits on him; he is a completely independent agent. He is also not liable for product sales. That may sound contradictory, but what that means is that you cannot hold them liable beyond discontinuing business with them. A broker is not a collections department, either. There are definite limits to what you can expect from a broker.
A broker is a representative of your brand for as long as you hold an agreement with him or her, but that same broker will also be a representative of other brands that they are trying to place. When it comes down to it, a broker is a well-connected (hopefully) agent who facilitates sales of products.

There are different sizes and different types of brokers. There are brokers who are very small and may work out of a small office or even out of their home. There are also large brokerage firms with brokers doing upwards of $500 million or even a billion dollars in sales in the U.S. and abroad. In the U.S. there are several very large brokers like Acosta, or Advantage Sales and Marketing (the largest broker in the U.S.

right now). Advantage has expanded into Canada as well by buying out a brokerage firm there.

How Brokers Work

Hopefully now you understand a little about what a broker is; now you need to know how they work.

On the basic level, there is very little that you need to do for a broker that you are not already doing. Once you locate a broker and reach an agreement with them, he will add your product to the portfolio and begin presenting it on your behalf to potential buyers—distributors and retailers. The broker then collects the orders and turns the buyer over to you.

Some brokers will offer additional services, and some will offer them, but for an additional fee. For example, some brokers will take care of all the paperwork that is required to register the brand, register the pricing, and all the other forms (which are many) required to sell the product into the retail account. Others, as described above, just secure the target and turn it over to you with all the documentation and terms and agreements. They do, however, comply the customer and stay in constant contact with them and handle their orders. You would receive a fax or an email with a purchase order that has been represented by the broker, and he or she earns their commission based on that sale.

Contracting with a Broker

The agreement is similar to the contract that you might sign with a distributor. It is a legally binding document that lays out the broker's function and responsibility, and also details terms for payment and compensation. This will be a commission agreement whereby you pay something between a 2.5% and 20% commission on the sale price of the product to the retailer or distributor.

A broker contract is a document of protection, too, just like the distributor contract is. It offers protection for both you and the broker. The contract will protect the broker's account for a span of months or years. The industry norm at the time being includes a 30 day cancellation clause, which gives you the right to end the arrangement with 30 days notice. After that time what happens to those accounts will depend on the agreement and how savvy the broker was. An experienced broker will include provisions so that they continue to collect commissions on the accounts they opened for several months or years, and sometimes indefinitely for as long as you sell to that client.

The agreement will also list payments terms, which are on average 15 to 30 days to the broker after funds are received from the buyer (retailer or distributor). If payment is not received, it is the responsibility of you or your accounts receivable department (although you can leverage the relationship of the broker with the buyer and his inability to get paid until payment is received to lend his additional weight to the matter).

The larger brokers will not come free; they will charge a fee to get listed with them. That fee can range up to $20,000 for the bigger brokerage houses. This is a fee that helps them cover the costs of getting sales moving, but also one designed as protection for the broker, to make sure you are serious about your business and about maintaining a relationship with them. Working strictly on commission with nothing binding you to the broker would put that agent in a tenuous position and make it all too easy for manufacturers to come and go and leave them without a source of income. Additionally, there may be additional fees for additional services, so you will want to know what your money is paying for upfront, and what remains your responsibility. The fees for smaller brokers will be smaller, or may not even be charged, but do be aware that that is a common and reasonable practice.

What a Broker Needs From You

You cannot assume that just because you have a product a broker will willingly represent it. Like distributors, brokers can have their pick of products with all the beverages that are out there. Also like distributors, and like retailers, too, the broker's job only goes so far—you are still, always, ultimately responsible for the support that makes the sales.

In order to make those sales the broker will need you to provide sales literature, front line pricing, brochures, and all the information included in your retailer and distributor packages so that they can represent that and convey to buyers that this product has the necessary support. These are not things you can expect the broker to develop for you, with the exception of a few inexperienced brokers who have not realized that that is not their burden and some others who offer it as an additional service because they know how to put those things together and know having them helps their cause. By and large, though, brokers do not create the retailer and distributor packages.

Samples are not the responsibility of the broker, either. Instead, the broker will make his contacts and provide you with a list of clients who are expecting product to sample. You then need to get those samples out to them—which means you continue to bear that work, and also that cost. It's one more thing to be aware of and plan for.

If you do not support your product or fund your product, or do not follow through with your end, you will find that very quickly your product just lies dormant in the broker's portfolio. Before you go out and contact brokers, you need to have all of these pieces in place, including proper funding, or they will either a)outright refuse you, or b) accept your product and your fee paid, but go nowhere with your sales.

You may have noticed that there can be a lot of variables when working with brokers. It is important to make sure each of these is clear to all parties, and to give your broker the tools that he needs to make your sales by holding up your end.

Why Use a Broker?

Brokers often come to be brokers after having some other experience in a related business, such as a category buyer for a chain or a large store (many of the smaller brokers in particular get their start this way). The end result is that the broker builds a large network of connections with other brokers, retailers, and distributors. This lends a great deal of outreach to your business. Obviously, the larger firms have an even greater outreach, if working with one is within your budget's funding.

That outreach is one reason to go with a broker. Another would be the work that is performed on your behalf, which you do not pay for unless results are realized. For smaller start-up companies brokers are a great way to start out and get into retailers and distributors that otherwise will not talk to you. Many brokers have been working with these contacts for many, many years and can basically walk product into any account and get feedback from them. The added benefit is that these buyers have trustworthy, open relationships with the buyers and won't waste their time; they'll be frank and honest about what products have potential, and vice-versa (meaning that buyers trust the opinions of brokers not to lead them into a product that cannot profit, so they will readily sign onto a sale).

On the downside, there is obviously an additional level of cost involved when you work with brokers, and a bad, unskilled, or unmotivated broker may sit on your product without ever pushing it, and may cost you sales. Care in choosing and clearly defined contracts helps ensure a profitable arrangement for all involved.

Some Notes on Choosing the Right Broker

Before we leave this discussion on brokers, we want to add a few notes about working with them and choosing brokers.

There are brokers for all kinds of products, and like distributors there are those who specialize in beverage and those who run an entire portfolio of diverse and sometimes unrelated products. Those types of brokers will not generally do a great job of selling your drink because they are basically a Jack-of-All-Trades, master of none.

Also, much as a big broker may seem the obvious way to go, there is potential for failure there, too. Many of the large brokerage houses have all the top brands listed, and will focus 80% of their attention on them, leaving your product to collect dust on a shelf.

Another problem that comes up is that some of these large brokers are working with the biggest of retail chains and accounts, and focus on those big-name retailers. But when it is time to fill in the gaps and sell to the smaller stores and independent accounts, they are not willing to devote their time to what they view as less profitable avenues.

These are things to be wary of as you structure your agreements with these brokers. Many will expect the same kind of exclusivity that a distributor will, but you have to build-in a safeguard so that if they do not move your product, and do not go after all the accounts, there is a window built in so that you can bring in other brokers to service them and net those sales.

Brokers can be an excellent sales mechanism for your beverage, if you know how to manage the relationship, and if you attend to all of your responsibilities. It is definitely to your advantage to know about brokers and know all of this ahead of time, so that you can consider it as you build your business plan, and your business empire!

The Ultimate in Sales Success: Selling to Consumers

Finally, we've reached the pinnacle of success for your new age beverage—successful sales to the consumer market.

It may seem that we've come a long way, and that your work is nearly done, and it is true we've learned a lot, but as work goes, you are never done until you have made that sale to volumes of end consumers—to your all-too-important target market. Selling to retailers and distributors is only the start of sales; the real work comes in selling off the shelves to consumers. Do that, and your work with retailers and distributors will be easy. They'll love you, they'll love your product, and they'll buy it by the truckload.

How to Sell to Consumers

There are dozens of books on how to sell to consumers. We'll focus on beverages, and on traditional beverage sales using distributors and retailers instead of drop shipping, Multi-Level Marketing or direct sales. One thing you need to put above all else when selling you should bring from the marketing chapter. Make an emotional connection with your consumer.

Your actual vehicle for selling to consumers will depend on your target market. It has to reflect their wants and needs.

When it comes down to it, sales to consumers are a matter of connection and visibility. You need to make your product known to them, and utilize marketing tactics to help them get to know it better. We are going to go over the four major potentials for achieving that goal.

Advertising

Advertising for a new beverage presents an interesting dilemma; it is something of a chicken and an egg problem, where the question becomes, What comes first? The advertising or the distribution?
The answer is simpler than you think. It is the distribution. There is a mantra we repeat quite frequently here at Liquid Brands Management, and it is one to live by—

No promotion without distribution!

You can't spend any money in promotion if people cannot find your product to buy. And the way people find your product is by having it in the stores. But how do you get around this? Didn't we just spend the better part of two chapters emphasizing the importance of product support, and its importance to distributors and retailers? How can you create a retailer or a distributor package without advertising in place?

For starters, know that any advertising that you do has to be local to the territory that you have opened. It also has to know limits; if you do not have the distribution in place, you have to place limits on the amount of advertising you do. You have to be very conservative because advertising dollars can be spent very, very quickly with no result. It can get out of hand very quickly.

You should be aware though, that as soon as people see your product listed you will begin to get calls for advertising. You need to resist the temptation to jump at every opportunity before you. Those opportunities come at a high cost.

Getting back to the problem at hand, it is possible to tie your advertising into your business plan and sales revenues. The way to do this is to allocate that percentage of sales, and allocate funding that is reliant on sales targets being met. In other words, once you have sold X number of cases, you will begin advertising campaign A, and once the next sales target of sales is met, campaign B will kick off. For example, you might set a target of opening 150 accounts, and once that target is met you will roll out radio advertising; with another 100, you will follow up with TV ads; 200 more and you do print ads and outdoor advertising; with the distributor's first order you agree to wrap their trucks, and you go on from there. Those sales targets should be tied into a number of cases that have been sold, delivered, and paid (not just delivered, because they could be returned and you could still have no revenue to pay for the advertising).

As long as you approach your distributors and retailers with a definitive, well-structured plan like this, they will have what they need to know that the advertising will be there if and when the targets are met. Advertising is a necessary part of the plan, but there have to be performance measures set so that it does not kill your product before it gets off the ground.

That tells you how and when to implement your advertising to consumers, but how do you know when to use each type? Not all kinds of advertising are appropriate all of the time, and not for all target markets. Radio, for instance, is appropriate for reaching some market segments, and not others. This is a matter of knowing your consumer and how they spend their time. Some spend a great deal listening to radio and hence radio ads, while others are more primarily a print or TV market. Your local advertising agency will help you define those targets (don't rely on the medium themselves—a TV producer will always think they are the way to go!).

Print is another option, but it is usually one that you want to rely on more for those promotions and sales. Print advertising for beverages is most commonly in sales flyers, or includes a coupon or something that promotes a special in one form or another.

Outdoor advertising—like signs, freeway signs, and billboards—is one of those formats that you want to reserve for after distribution is in place (one to tie to a number of accounts) because the audience is a mobile audience. That distribution needs to be large, because 60% of that audience will not be local to you; so unless they are pulling over right now to buy your drink, they will not find it in the stores once they get home. You may have just spent several thousand dollars toward a consumer that will probably not have any chance of finding your product.

Sponsorships

As a product producer you will have no shortage of opportunities to give money away in sponsorships in return for some visibility; if well-placed, that can definitely sell to your desired group of consumers. But like advertising, sponsorships can get very expensive very quickly, but if there is no sales or distribution you have no means of supporting that sponsorship.

The amount of money that you spend sponsoring an athlete, entertainer, motocross rider, or event will be tied to the number of eyes that are on it—on their exposure. An event that will be watched by 10 million people will cost a lot of money. You can see how a professional athlete or large event will be very expensive, because there will be a large viewership and a high level of exposure. Celebrity players and figures are also in the media, increasing the exposure of your logo and advertising every time they are photographed with your hat or t-shirt on. Expense aside, you also have to have your distribution and brand recognition to even get these big names to sign with you—they all have an image, an income, and a name to uphold, and they will not cheapen that by going with a no-name drink no one can find.

That basically speaks to large sponsorships, but there are other sponsorships that should not be discounted. Schools and community sports and groups are a great place to start. Colleges and universities are ideal for products with that age-group as their target, especially because these younger groups can provide buyers for generations. They're also more willing to try a new product. These smaller groups are always in need of sponsors, and the cost is significantly lower than jumping into the big names. Starting a small, grass-roots campaign like this can build trust and recognition that serves as a solid foundation for upward growth and sales.

Sampling Events

Sampling events are different than in-store sampling, but they are still highly consumer-focused. Sampling events work well in local settings, such as at local community or charity events. Typically these will be events that are geared to the average consumer or to a group with a specific group or team in mind. You will need to gauge how appropriate that outreach is for your drink.

You will need several things to get into and operate at a sampling event of this sort. If you are opening packages and serving beverage you will probably need a local food handler's permit, or someone on the staff will, and you'll have to see to that before the event. You will also need practical supplies, like tents, t-shirts or uniforms for staff, tables, cups, and trash receptacles; and you will need product—lots of product. You have to make sure if you do this that you do it well, and consumers are serviced well so they think well of you when they walk away.

This all sounds like a lot of work and investment to give your product away (unless you are lucky enough to be involved in a situation where the event can actually be used for selling, but that is not the norm). It is. What's the return for you, then?

- Brand exposure
- Ideally, connection with your target market, or a portion of it
- Potentially extended exposure at long-lasting/day events
- Exposure to a full range of consumers across all ages (depending on the event, unless a very targeted, identified crowd)

These are great benefits when they are well-planned, but you need to take care in selecting the sampling events that you agree to do so that you can maximize that exposure and advantage.

Night Club Events

Another possibility for reaching your consumer is night club events. Night clubs are a great place to get a product exposed, but do keep in mind that they are not a great place to get product sales. This is not a place where you will generate a lot of sales for your product. Here's why—if you have a night club and they pack it in with a thousand people, that is a thousand people with all sorts of different choice products and tastes. Not everybody is going to try your product or mix it in with their liquor of choice. A night club event may result in a few sales, but if you choose to do one you should do it for the large exposure potential, and not for sales on the spot. That is precisely what most of the brands that are doing night club events are using them for. Because the vast majority of the sales and product used is alcohol, these just will not generate the sales for you as a retail choice.

This, basically, is sales to consumers. It is the most important part of your business, but it is actually very basic. You need to get your product in front of those consumers, and you need to get them interested, and committed to your drink. Basic though it may be, that does not mean that you can afford not to attend to it or to let it lapse. Selling consumers will always be priority for your product, and it is an area that you will need to attend to consistently and on an ongoing basis.

Conclusion

....

It's been quite a journey, but we've done it. We've gone through every aspect of the Beverage business, and come out the other side. You are now well on your way to profiting in this promising, growing business.

Journey to Success

You have journeyed with us through each part of the beverage world. You've learned about that world and about the opportunities it is simply bursting with; the opportunities that are waiting for you to capitalize on them, with a level of success unknown to the average drink developer.

You've gone through the entire process, from start to finish, of developing your product and positioning it for maximum sales and profits. You've learned how to get your drink produced, attending to every last detail right down to the seemingly inconsequential cap on the bottle (of course, we know the reality of the importance of those finer details...).

Finally, you've come to learn the most important lessons in the business—how to plan, market, and sell your drink through every avenue, to every critical party. How to plan for success and make it a reality!

I know going through a text such as this requires commitment and dedication. Thank you for spending all this time with us. We want to hear from you. Tell us about your projects, your company, ideas, or what you think of this book. You can contact us through the website, phone, or social media.

Diligence, Rewarded

We appreciate your diligence in staying with us through this journey, and on to the end. We know that this patience and dedication will mean all the difference to you and your business and future. Because of it, you are at a tremendous advantage over others who have tried and failed, and continue to try and fail without the right level of knowledge and planning. That knowledge and planning is yours now, the most solid foundation we could possibly provide for a sustainable, profitable, valuable Beverage business.

Continuing Support for Success

A new venture takes a lot of time and effort, many times a whole lot of money. Make sure you use education as one of the tools to cut the amount of effort, time and money you need for your business. If you're launching a brand or a business read as many books as you can on marketing, branding, sales and management. Listen to audios, go see some webinars and speak to as many people in the industry you can.

When I decided to put the effort into the business world, first as an executive, then as an entrepreneur, I read up to one hundred books per year, yes. This is after reading a book a day for many years on other subjects. If two books per week is a bit of an overkill for you consider that you'll have to spend thousands of hours and hundreds of thousands of dollars in your business. I recommend you get addicted to audio books and listen to them while you drive, exercise, walk, and whenever you're not on the phone.

Consume as much information as you can. It will not only make you better in business, it will improve your knowledge, communication, and relationships.

As part of a continuing support for the success of executives and entrepreneurs, I provide free webinars, audios, podcasts, case studies and much more. Just visit www.BuildYourBeverageEmpire.com and subscribe to the newsletter to get emails on new events.

Please stay in touch, send me your beverage photos to share with other readers on my blogs and social media pages. It's free advertising for you to more than 100,000 followers and many retailers and distributors that can buy your products. I love to hear from readers that launched a new product, or got a new distributor, or landed a new VP job at a major soda company. Just go to my website and shoot me an email or share on social media.

As a final word, Carlos and I would like to offer you our congratulations. It is no small task to complete this journey, and you are to be congratulated for embarking on it. You are also to be congratulated for your foresight in picking a winning opportunity. We hope to see each and every one of you become a raging success in the Beverage market; and so our last word is this—Good luck to you as you **Build Your Beverage Empire!**

Glossary of
Beverage Terms

....

CSD: Carbonated Soft Drink (mainly soda, but now energy drinks are counted in the category.)

C-store: Convenience store

Drop-shipping: a method of product direct delivery that does not rely on a distributor or retailer; product is shipped directly from the producer's warehouse to the retailer through an outside delivery company

DSD: Direct Store Delivery; product is delivered directly to the retail location without first passing through a distributor or warehouse. Typically delivery is handled by an outside company specializing in delivery of packages such as the postal service, UPS, FedEx, or another transport company.

Foodservice: refers to entities within the service industry, such as institutional kitchens, restaurants, bars, or companies servicing them (such as a foodservice distributor providing product and supplies to those retailers)

Mass Retail: large chain retail accounts making smaller sales directly to consumers; refers primarily to pharmacy and supermarket retail chains

Merchandising: Refers to efforts undertaken to promote product within the retail location—presence/use of POP/POS materials, and also efforts such as inventory and stocking. Can also refer to the marketing concepts behind the actions.

New Age Beverage: a consumer drink that is not included in any of the traditional categories of beverage; includes teas, energy drinks, new sodas, vitamin drinks, specialty waters, and others. Typically does not refer to traditional carbonated beverages and sodas or fruit juices

New Soda: a more healthful version of carbonated soft drink developed by traditional soda producers as a foothold into the NAB market

Point: percentage points of a sale

POP: Point of Purchase. See POS, Point of Sale

POS: Point of Sale, also called "Point of Purchase". Refers to marketing tactics and materials used in the retail location at the place where consumers will see and buy your product. Includes advertising materials such as posters, stickers, signs, and price clings

On-premise: accounts where product is consumed on-site. Includes retail locations such as restaurants and bars, clubs, foodservice providers

SKU: a unique number or identifier assigned to a product for the purposes of scanning for sales, ordering, and delivery (also referred to as a bar-code

Spiff: commissions paid on product sold organized into a program meant to work as an incentive to sales teams, usually for the sales force of the distributor

Turns: volume of sales in a wholesale or retail market; for example, the number of times your product is sold and reordered by the same retailer or distributor (measured in a consistent volume, such as case, pallet, etc.)

3 Step System of Distribution: full-service distribution process wherein the distributor collects retail orders, fulfills them (delivers product), and stocks and merchandises the product

Warehouse Program: A method of selling directly to retailers without going through a distributor wherein retailers use their own distribution network

Wholesalers: Large distributors who do not specialize in beverages (or any one product), but sell many different products to a variety of distributors and retailers

Table of Figures

Index

E

F

G

H

I

L

M

R

S

T

U

V

More Content or Coaching

Beverage Industry Domination

Your next step in the quest for beverage domination is sales and distribution or coaching.

If you're ready to get your product into Mass Retail Accounts all over the USA go directly to the course:
www.WholesaleMBA.com/course

If you need help from me now; in coaching, mentoring and consulting, call today in the USA:

USA Phone: +1 (619) 730-1473